Pink Trees Press

For Jersey Boy
John
I think you'll like the
SOMERDALE section in PARTICULAR

Best
Phillip
2/13/2023

Good Boy,

Bad Boy,

A Better Man

A Cautionary Tale

Word on the Street

Phillip Giambri's new work transports the reader to a world bathed in the elegance of simplicity—where words are as crisp and clean as freshly washed sheets on a clothesline in a summer breeze. Memories laid bare ripple in our thoughts well beyond the moment they are taken in. It's a deviation from Giambri's earlier works where his ever-evolving voice now steps in with a palpable authenticity as if to make certain that the author has a far more tender heart than he'd ever fully allowed one to see. In *Good Boy, Bad Boy, A Better Man*, Giambri opens a new door where we meet a better man indeed. –Marie Sabatino, Writer/Storyteller

In Phillip Giambri's most recent collection of vivid prose vignettes *Good Boy, Bad Boy, A Better Man,* a lost world is recalled in the tradition of Jack Kerouac as the Great Rememberer. With the skilled practitioner of the art of the spoken word set to robust prose, these word picture snapshots cut with an uncluttered precision of a master storyteller. From some of Phillip's earliest memories as a child growing up in urban Philadelphia to an emerging adult on the lower east side of NYC, one can travel back to a lifetime of personal pivotal touchstones that vibrate, resonate, entertain, and delight. -Vincent Quatroche, Author, Q Bop City – Poet/Storyteller

Curious reality readers will respond to the universal connections of emotions and memories that Phillip Giambri shares with us in his new memoir *Good Boy, Bad Boy, A Better Man*. After reading his book for the third time I realize it's a love story, written by a receiver and a hunter of love and the broken fragments of it that shine like diamonds on the sticky gunk of an old linoleum floor. -Ezra Lovecroft, Poet.

Phillip Giambri's stories are funny, fascinating, and real; a taste of an age long past. Characters like Charlie the Goat Man, Uncle Leon, Farmer Dobbs all cast a spell—that resonates far beyond the page. Don't miss this book—it's a treasure! -Ted Krever, Author *Swindler and Son: A Heist Misadventure*

Phillip Giambri's new book *Good Boy, Bad Boy, A Better Man,* offers vignettes of his memories; snippets of his past, and how it connects to the future. A childhood with innocence and angst flowing into challenging and carefree adulthood and how one man ambitiously changed with the times. With vivid descriptions, I found myself traveling with Phillip, walking in step with him as he navigated multiple careers, loves, and places he has lived. -Qurrat Kadwani, Writer/Actress

Titles from Pink Trees Press

Origami Book #1, Linda Kleinbub
Origami Book #2, Linda Kleinbub
Silver Tongued Devil Anthology, Linda Kleinbub &
Anthony C. Murphy, Editors
Poems from an Unending Pandemic, Phillip Giambri
Dysfunction: A Play on Words in the Familiar, Pauline Findlay
Good Boy, Bad Boy, A Better Man, Phillip Giambri

Good Boy,

Bad Boy,

A Better Man
A Cautionary Tale

by
Phillip Giambri

Pink Trees Press
New York City

Cover Art by Linda Wulkan

Acknowledgments

"Charlie's Log Cabin Inn" and a portion of "Drinkin' My Dolphins" previously appeared in the 2016 book "Confessions of a Repeat Offender".

Big thanks to Pink Trees for putting their imprimatur on my book and working to get it published.

Special thanks to Linda Kleinbub and Madeline Artenberg, my editors, for supporting my work and for their tireless quest for editing perfection.

Cover art by Linda Wulkan.

Library of Congress Control Number: 2022911907
ISBN: 978-15136-9471-9

**Dedicated
to
Family
(blood and chosen)
and
Life Loves
(past and present)**

Contents

Why This Book?

This book did not happen the way I intended. I began putting together a book of previously unpublished stories and poems, but my muse seems to have had other plans.

Most of my written work is dictated to me by a voice in my head that I call my Muse. I seldom write anything that she hasn't directly dictated. I may not hear from her for months or even years at a time, and during that time, nothing gets written. She usually chooses to visit around five in the morning when she wakes me with a story or poem. When I get up, I write it down because, at this point, I've learned to trust her judgment. I've published four books dictated mostly by her. I'm happy with them and people seem to like them.

As I begin outlining the stories in a timeline, she keeps waking me each morning with more additions and inserts. Memories are brought back to my earliest childhood and I relive many beautiful life moments along with more than enough embarrassing and ugly memories. I dutifully recorded them all and rearranged the timelines.

I'm not including dive bar stories, love affairs, or specific military memories that were previously published as stories or poems in my books *Confessions of a Repeat Offender* and *The Amorous Adventures of Blondie and Boho: Two East Village Dive Bar Coyotes*.

I started as a good kid, but as a teen and into my twenties, turned bad. I started gettin' my shit together in my thirties, leveled off, and since then, have been mostly nice. At some point in my mid-thirties, I realized that the life I was living was largely an angry rebellion against my father who I seemed never able to please when young. Light bulb over the head moment: *"He's still controlling you if your life is centered on rebellion against him, asshole. Time to start living your own life."*

That moment in my mid-thirties was when I let go of the anger that controlled most of my earlier life and I began a new life. I find joy now in my own choices rather than choices made in anger and opposition. Life has become quite good and I'm at peace with myself. It's really hard for anyone to piss me off anymore. I'm too busy doing what makes me happy so I won't make time to participate in someone else's anger trip.

I hope that my story identifies moments that others have experienced or shared and can offer a universal connection of emotions and memories that touch people.

My life and my story are no better or worse than anyone else's but I hope that putting it to paper has opened my heart honestly enough to allow others to see, feel, and love life the way I do.

The book covers my life from my beginnings in the early 40s until I'm in my mid-thirties and meet my future wife in the 70s. Any inaccuracies found on names, places, dates, or people are certainly not deliberate and cannot be blamed on my muse. She did the best she could using the memory tools she had to deal with at my extreme age. I'm guessin' we're about 95% accurate on details .... and maybe a bit fictionalized to cover memory lapses and/or possible lawsuits.

Good Boy

"A boy's story is the best that is ever told."
-Charles Dickens

Giambri's Market on the corner of Mifflin and Camac Streets 1926
Grandfather Filippo, grandmother Salvatora, and son Joseph Giambri along with
neighbors.

Our Street, Our House: 1941-1953

On Camac Street in the 1940s, gas street lamps are lit at dusk by city Lamp Lighters, who carry wooden ladders on their rounds lighting each lamp on their route. City Street Sweepers clean our street with large brooms, followed by metal trash cans mounted on wheels and pushed by men who shovel into the cans manure, garbage, and trash left by service horses, wagons, merchants, hucksters, and careless neighbors.

In South Philadelphia, Camac Street, between 12th and 13th is very narrow with tiny row houses. Most have two or three front steps made of white marble. Every Saturday morning, the ladies of Camac Street clean their marble front steps with scrubbing brushes and Ajax powdered cleanser. It's a Philadelphia tradition. Our house is one of the

few without marble steps. The front of our house was remodeled at some earlier time with new brick facing and brick steps.

Like many of our neighbors, our cheap wooden front door is artfully painted and varnished by a local street artist to look like dark, grained, knotted, wood. We have a coal heater and minimal hot water. A large unheated kitchen with a room above it was added to the house before we moved in.

Pastina

I'm in a highchair in our kitchen. My mom's father, Antonio, walks toward me carrying a small grey porcelain pot with white dots on it. He's warmed up a lunch of pastina soup and spoon-feeds me. My grandfather dies in May of 1943 just before I'm two years old. This is my earliest memory.

Bomb's Away

I'm terrified during World War II air-raid drills with loud sirens blaring in the night. I squeeze into the small space in the corner behind the refrigerator and close my eyes. Mom and Dad pull down blackout shades and curtains to block light from being seen by enemy bombers. Not many years later, I'll be curled up under my school desk to practice protecting myself from an atomic bomb blast. Things don't change much.

Hubba Hubba, Ding Ding!

South Philly is home to the Philadelphia Naval Shipyard and the Philadelphia Naval Hospital. During WWII and after, our streets are overflowing with sailors whose ships are in for repair or are in treatment at the Naval Hospital. They always seem to be hugging or holding hands with pretty young girls. Sailors often whistle at and cat-call my mother with "Hubba hubba, ding ding!" when she's wheeling me around in my stroller. These images and the

Cracker Jack sailor uniforms are imprinted in my brain and plant the seeds of my desire to be a sailor. Mom and Dad buy me a sailor suit near the end of the war and it's just like the one real sailors wear. They have my picture taken with me smiling in my sailor suit. I'm a sailor boy.

A Big Yellow Taxi

Mom and I are at Woolworth's on Broad Street and I'm having a screaming temper tantrum because mom won't buy me a cast-iron, yellow toy taxicab. I carry on screaming and crying until a stranger comes over and asks mom why she won't buy me the toy. Embarrassed, Mom admits she can't afford it. He buys the taxi and hands it to me. She thanks him, but is clearly upset. When he leaves, she grabs the taxi and gives me "The Look" which I see many times over the years. I call it "The Chicken Eye" because it's a cold stare that looks like the eyes of a dead chicken.

When we get home, mom puts the toy taxi high up on a cabinet in the kitchen where I can see it but not reach it. I'm never allowed to play with that toy taxi. Lesson learned, don't mess with mom!

Johnny Comes Marchin' Home

So many young men enlist in World War II from our draft district that married men with children are exempted, including my father, my uncle Eugene, and my uncle Leon. All of my father's cousins, his brother, and most of his

21

friends go off to fight in the war. All but one come back safe. Dad's cousin Sammy is a B-17 bomber pilot. He survives thirty-five missions over Germany, only to die in a training crash in Texas near the war's end.

When boys from Camac Street come home, the street is closed off and we have a "block party" celebrating their safe return. The street is decorated with flags and bunting and everyone sets a table in front of their home offering food and drink. There's music, songs, and couples swing-dancing all day. We're proud of our boys and grateful for their return.

We kids endlessly run up and down the street eating food, playing games, and hugging our soldiers. My uncle Nick, still in uniform, hoists me up on his shoulders and parades around with me waving, as he shakes hands and is embraced by our friends and neighbors.

I find it strange now that so many Italian Americans in WWII were sent to fight in Italy, their ancestral home. Some of my relatives were sent to North Africa for the invasion of Sicily and fought their way north through all of Italy until marching into Berlin in 1945 with General Patton's Army.

The House on Mifflin

Our neighborhood is almost exclusively Sicilian. My father's parents live on the corner of Camac and Mifflin Streets and own a grocery store. My grandfather works in his store for fifty years and never bothers to learn much English because everyone speaks Sicilian. My grandmother, on the other hand, speaks English fluently with barely a trace of an accent.

Grandmom and Grandpop live in back of and above the store. Behind the store is a small parlor with a staircase to the second floor. Past the parlor is a large kitchen. Outside the kitchen is a yard and a "summer kitchen."

I love to bathe here because there's always very hot water, not like our house. Sometimes I get to watch Grandpop shave in the morning. He swooshes his shaving brush around in the shaving soap bowl and lathers up his face. He opens his straight razor and strokes it back and forth on a strop that hangs next to the mirror. He slowly pulls the razor across his face. As he shaves, it makes a scratching sound as it cuts away at his beard. He frequently dips the razor in hot water to clean off suds and hair. I'm mesmerized watching him shave. I want to grow up and have a beard so I can put suds on my face and shave like Grandpop.

A-Bombs and Friday Night Fights

My grandparents are the first in our neighborhood to have a 12" Philco TV in the late 40s. After school, I sit in their parlor watching test patterns until the Atomic Bomb Tests come on live and I stare in amazement as giant mushroom clouds form. Soldiers in uniforms, wearing sunglasses, and model houses, positioned nearby for the tests, are battered by strong winds and a blinding light from the bomb blasts.

I also watch the Kefauver Crime Committee Hearings, not because I'm at all interested or know what they're about, but because it's on television and it's amazing to watch real people talking from far away. It seems like magic to me.

Neighbors gather outside my grandparent's parlor window on Friday nights to watch the Gillette Friday Night Fights live on television.

Video Killed the Radio Star

Except for the newspaper, radio is our primary source of news and entertainment. My mom and her sister Margie love the Bob Hope radio show. They sit listening on the floor staring at the radio and clap with excitement when the Lux Radio Theater comes on. Dad listens to news and commentary by Gabriel Heatter and Edward R. Murrow. I'm totally addicted to kid's radio serials, close my eyes, and become part of the stories: The Lone Ranger, Bobby Benson & The B-Bar-B Riders, Superman, Martin Kane-Private Eye, and The Shadow. My favorite is Bobby Benson 'cause he's a kid like me and I follow his daily adventures as if I were him. I know I'll be a cowboy someday too.

When we finally get a TV, I'm so disappointed when I see Superman and The Lone Ranger for the first time. They look like normal people and not the superheroes I imagine from the radio and comic books.

TV is a major disappointment for me until the Howdy Doody show comes on. Buffalo Bob, Clarabell, Howdy, Mr. Bluster, Flub-a-Dub, and all the others are fun, the stories are great,

24

and I'm in love with Princess Summerfall Winterspring. I'm heartbroken when I learn she died in a car accident. She's quickly replaced on the show but it's never the same again for me.

Colored Easter Chicks

Mom buys us four dyed Easter chicks at Woolworths: baby blue, pink, deep purple, and canary yellow. We house them in a small cardboard box in the kitchen with sawdust on the bottom and a light clipped to the box to keep them warm in our cold kitchen. We love these chicks, feed them, and care for them until they grow so large, that we have to put them in a big empty Scott's toilet paper box, which stands about three-feet high and three-feet square. The chicks are rapidly becoming chickens and are healthy and loud. One morning, we come down for breakfast to find that rats have chewed holes in the box, killed the chickens, dismembered them, and eaten pieces of them. There are body parts, blood, and feathers strewn around the kitchen. My sister Doris and I are hysterical. It's gonna take years to get over that trauma.

Italian Allstars

Most of the baseball and boxing stars in the late 40s and 50s are Italian-Americans. Our mostly Sicilian-immigrant community loves them, supports them, listens to games and boxing matches daily on the radio, and watches them on TV whenever possible. On the corner of Camac Street in the next block is the Passyunk Gym. Every Saturday afternoon, my dad takes me to watch the boxing champions who come to the gym to train for upcoming fights in Philly. I meet Rocky Marciano, Rocky Graziano, Joey Giardello, Joey Giambra, and many other notable Italian boxers of that era. Expected to die at any time from tuberculosis, my dad vicariously lives his dream life in sports through

the many Italian-American sports stars, especially boxers.

Just an Athletic Supporter

I'm about six years old and I get a pair of boxing gloves for Christmas. Dad spends endless hours teaching me to throw jabs, hooks, body shots, and how to bob and weave to avoid punches. About once a month, we go to my Aunt Jean's house and I have to box my cousin Bobby. He's two years older, four or five inches taller, and has a much longer reach than me. I mostly bob and weave, trying to avoid getting hit without throwing many punches. Bobby is always declared the winner. Dad mentions that I don't seem to have good hand/eye coordination. I have no idea what that means, but sports become my nemesis.

As I get older, I find that in neighborhood stickball, baseball, or touch football games, I'm always the last one to be chosen, usually with a line like, "Well, I guess we got Phillip."

My apparent lack of hand/eye coordination and poor performance in sports is a major disappointment to my father and begins a wedge between us that only widens over the years. I never seem capable of reaching the high expectations he's set for me.

That feeling of never being good enough for my peers and my dad will define my rebellious attitude and reactions to leaders and authority figures for many years to come.

The Sound of Music

Some Sunday mornings, we wake up to the sound of music. We rush to look out the front bedroom windows to see and hear *La Banda Bianca, The White Band.* On the anniversary of a family's arrival from Sicily, *The Banda Bianca* serenades under the windows of the family, playing beautiful Sicilian folk songs for them. Each band member is elegantly dressed in a pure white uniform with gold trim and gold buttons. Such a lovely tradition. The family being serenaded, and all the nearby neighbors, toss coins to the sidewalk in gratitude.

Autumn: Dago Red and Scooters

In Autumn, there are no falling leaves on Camac Street. There are no trees. The sidewalks and curbs are lined and stacked high with cases of crushed grapes, the remnants of extensive home winemaking. My family buys homemade wine for our dinners from our neighbors for $.25 a gallon. They also provide the wine for masses at St. Nicholas Church free of charge. Our Pastor, Father Fabrizzi, loves Camac Street wine and enjoys lots of it before, during, and after mass.

More important to me, Fall is also "Scooter Season" in South Philly. Each boy makes his own and I decorate mine with soda-bottle caps nailed all over the front and sides. Pretty snazzy ride.

The Fall air on Camac Street may lack the crisp smell of fallen leaves but it's filled with the bittersweet aroma of fermented grapes and the whoosh, whoosh, whooshing of boys on scooters.

The Dumps

On any given night, you can find cars parked vertically on Packer Avenue between Broad Street and 10th Street, with their headlights directed into the city dump. The car's passengers sit on fenders, hoods, and car roofs with rifles, mostly .22s, firing at the hundreds of rats scrambling for food under the daylight brightness of car headlights.

Garbage and trash collected by trash wagons and street sweepers are taken to the city's waste disposal site that everyone in South Philly calls, The Dumps.

Dad takes me to The Dumps to watch his brother Nick and friends shooting rats while they're sitting up on Grandpop's old Plymouth. It looks like a shooting gallery at a carnival except the targets are live rodents. Since everyone's firing at once, each person claims many more kills than they probably have so they all can feel like sharpshooters.

"I don't like this place. It stinks of rotten garbage and I don't wanna shoot rats. Let's go home, Dad."

Municipal Stadium

Municipal Stadium remains after the 1926 Exposition and is the largest stadium in the country, seating more than 100,00. The inner track around the football field is large enough to host Joey Chitwood Stock Car Races every summer. Our next-door neighbor drives the tow truck at the races and occasionally takes his two sons and me along to watch the races. He makes sure we sit high up in the stands because there are no guard rails or protective fencing. When cars are hit and go out of control, they leave the track and fly up into the stands at high speed, often hitting innocent people. It's exciting but pretty scary with the thunderous noise of unmufflered engines, thick blue smoke, the smell of burning rubber, and frequent crashes.

There are also Demolition Derbies where cars deliberately and continuously crash into each other until only one car is left still able to be driven. That's the winner. Seems pretty stupid. I only go twice. That's enough for me.

The Lakes

League Island Park is a man-made park designed for the Exposition. It's beautifully landscaped with numerous lakes, lots of grass, and trees. Everybody in

South Philly calls it "The Lakes," a favorite nighttime parking spot for couples to neck and maybe try for more.

Families spend weekend afternoons at The Lakes for picnicking, baseball, and touch football. There aren't many fish there anymore 'cause the water's pretty dirty. My dad says it's unsafe to eat anything you'd catch there.

I love The Lakes because, on the southernmost side of the park, there's a clear view of the warships docked at the Navy Yard. I love to look at them and dream of being a sailor someday.

Blonded by the Light

 Mom drags me kicking and screaming to Francis Read Elementary School and deposits me in Mrs. Donahue's first-grade classroom. I'm angry and upset and don't notice much or pay attention until recess when all the boys are asked to line up single file in the schoolyard and all the girls are asked to form a separate line alongside the boys. Lightning strikes when least expected. At the front of the girl's line stands a young girl with blue eyes and yellow hair. Never in my life have I ever seen anyone with other than dark brown or black hair. She stands calmly in front of the other girls in a halo of light and sparkling yellow hair. I am instantly lovestruck.

Marilyn Monroe will soon be called "The Blonde Bombshell," but for me, Dorothy Marchese is forever the only "Blonde Bombshell" I acknowledge. I ask mom how an Italian girl can have yellow hair and blue eyes. Mom says that Italians in Northern Italy are often lighter-skinned with blonde hair and blue eyes. I learn that her father owns a furniture store on Passyunk Avenue about two blocks from Camac Street. I often peek in the front window after school, hoping to catch a glimpse of my dream girl.

Dorothy and I spend six years in the same classrooms without her ever saying hello, speaking to me, or so much as acknowledging my existence. No matter. I leave unsigned Valentine cards on her desk every year but never have the courage to talk to her or let her know that the cards are from me. For six years, I stare at her endlessly in wonder and amazement, not able to imagine anyone more beautiful in the world. After graduating from Francis Read, I never see Dorothy again, but for the rest of my life, every fantasy of romance, love, sex, or marriage involves a beautiful blonde.

Penny Candy

There are two "penny candy" stores across the street from Francis Read on both the East and West corners of the school. Frank's specializes in exotic and fanciful candy, foods, and toys, like chewable wax lips and mustaches, candy dots on strips of paper, slices of Jewish pickles, and Chinese finger puzzles. If you're really flush, you can get a whole Jewish pickle for a nickel and secretly nibble on it

all afternoon in class. The main attraction at Frank's for a lot of boys is "loosies," two Lucky Strike cigarettes for a nickel. Most of us who toy with cigarettes just light them and puff smoke without inhaling. My classmate Harry smokes loosies around the corner from school

31

and even inhales them. He plays saxophone, never does homework, and always roams the streets with his coat open in the coldest weather. Miss Porter says he'll come to a bad end. I like Harry but think he's too wild to ever be friends with.

The other penny candy store on the East side of our school is Mrs. Ashley's, run by a genteel English lady who smells of perfume and powder. She sells more traditional chocolates, candy bars, licorice, pretzel rods, and sugar babies. At Mrs. Ashley's, I'm always well-behaved and extra nice because I think Mrs. Ashley would be offended by rudeness or bad behavior. I always smile and say thank you when she hands me my licorice or pretzel rod.

Home Alone with Aunt Jemima

I'm six or seven years old and Dad is mostly in and out of the sanitarium with TB. Mom works as a seamstress in a clothing factory to support us. My sister Doris and I are "latch key" kids during the school season. I have the house key tied to my belt loop with a long string and carefully stored in my front pants pocket.

On top of our refrigerator is an Aunt Jemima cookie jar. As far back as I remember, Mom always told us, that whenever we're home alone Aunt Jemima is watching everything we do and tells Mom when she comes home from work. We may suspect it isn't true but we're not willing to take any chances. We're very careful about anything we do or say within

Aunt Jemima's range of hearing or line of sight. We're sure she'd rat us out if what Mom says is true.

Teacher's Pet

I guess I compensate for Dorothy's lack of attention, and never seeming to be good enough to meet my dad's expectations, by seeking approval and ingratiating myself with the teachers. I learn to read and write before I start school so I begin a bit ahead of the other kids in class. I'm always first to raise my hand to answer questions, know the correct answers, and endlessly hope that Dorothy might notice me and be impressed. Dorothy never appears to notice but the other kids in class do. They make fun of me, and call me "Teacher's Pet."

During my six years at Francis Read, my grades are excellent, teachers all like me, but I don't have any friends. My close friends are the kids on my block and most of them go to Catholic school.

In fifth grade, my teacher Mr. Schwartz notices that I like reading history and science books. He privately asks if I know what Archeology is. When I tell him I've read about Egypt and the pyramids, he gives me a book called "Valley of the Kings" and I become obsessed with the thought of worldly adventures as an archeologist. He comments on my report card that he feels I have the potential to pursue a career in History and/or Archeology. My parents are impressed.

Mrs. McDermott comments the following year that I should be encouraged to pursue a career in writing.

Miss Porter, the mean spinster teacher hated by all students, comments on my report card that I have the potential to be the first Italian-American president of the United States.

My parents are elated, but to me, all that matters is my unrequited love for the elusive Dorothy Marchese. I leave Francis Read with high grades and a broken heart.

The Safety Patrol

Keystone Automobile Club and American Automobile Association (AAA) fund and support safety programs for elementary school boys. Keystone handles public schools and AAA handles Catholic schools. The Safety Patrol is designed to have young boys protect children and parents at street crossings near their school. Apparently, girls are not deemed capable or worthy enough to take on this tremendous responsibility in the late 40s. The Safety Patrol appeals to boys like me who crave attention or those with authoritarian tendencies.

In fifth grade, I join the Keystone Safety Patrol and am issued a three-inch-wide white canvas belt with a chrome twist-lock buckle and a white strap that runs from the center of the back, over the left shoulder, and down to the right hip. The large Keystone metal badge is worn heart-high on the crossover strap. It projects a military feeling and lets everyone know you're not just some punk kid on the street. I'm assigned a post on the corner of Sartain and McClellan Streets, just across from the school entrance. I'm there every day before and after school to ensure the safe passage of the students across either street. I stand facing the street and have been trained to raise my right arm for pedestrians to stop behind me until the street is clear of vehicles. When I lower my arm, they are safe to cross and I wave them on. All Safety Patrol boys are permitted to be fifteen minutes late for class and are allowed to leave fifteen minutes early at day's end to man their post.

I love the Safety Patrol. I love the attention, the feeling that I'm doing something important, helping people, and being respected by the teachers and principal. In sixth grade, I'm promoted to Lieutenant and responsible for making the rounds of all posts to ensure that a Patrol boy is covering them and there are no "slackers". By graduation, I've advanced to Safety Patrol Captain, make up the patrol assignments, and graduate smugly, knowing I've served my school well even if most of the kids think I'm a suck-up.

Donnie and Danger

In the late 40s and early 50s, there are lots of service horses working the streets of Philadelphia. Milk wagons, bread wagons, trash wagons, hucksters, and coal wagons are still mostly horse-drawn. There's a large watering trough around the corner from Camac Street that can water four horses at a time. You can still rent a horse on Washington Avenue to ride the streets of Philly.

Donnie is crazy about horses. Like me, he's an Italian-American kid who lives in South Philly during the school year and spends summers at his grandmother's home in Somerdale, NJ, where we meet and become friends. Donnie is two years older than me, is going through puberty, and is big for his age. He works at one of the rental stables after school and is an expert rider. His favorite horse is named Danger because he's ornery, not your average-rental-stable "hack" horse, and requires a high level of skill to ride. He's not available for rental, except to very experienced riders.

I don't usually see much of Donnie during the school year when I'm in Philly, but on a seemingly ordinary day when leaving Francis Read at 3:30, I find Donnie mounted on Danger, waiting in the schoolyard for me. He waves, motions me over, reaches out for my hand, and pulls me up on the back of the horse. I wrap my arms around his waist while looking at my schoolmates with what I can only describe now as a "see-how-cool-I-am" smile. The kids in the schoolyard stare in disbelief as Donnie spins Danger around and we gallop off down the street to my house a few blocks away, with me yelling, "Hi, ho, Silver, away!" We talk and catch up for a bit and Donnie says he has to get back to the stable 'cause he's working. I don't see Donnie again until school is out and we're both summering at our grandmother's homes in New Jersey. I'll never forget the feeling of fear, excitement, and satisfaction knowing the kids at Francis Read might finally think I'm cool. Sadly, it doesn't happen, but Donnie thinks I'm cool and that's good enough for this twelve-year-old, 'cause we're both gonna be cowboys someday.

A Room of My Own

I share a bedroom with my sister Doris next to my parents' bedroom until she reaches puberty. Poking around in her dresser drawers, I find a brassiere, wave it in her face, laugh, and ask what it's for, as she has no noticeable breasts. Neither my sister nor mom thinks it's funny so I'm hurriedly hustled off to the unheated back room, which will now be my bedroom. Before I inhabited this room, my parents had rented it to an elderly couple named Leo and Eleanor, who lived with us for several years and shared our bathroom and kitchen. It seemed perfectly normal to me at that very young age. My parents needed the money, I guess.

The windows in my new bedroom are loose, separated from the frames, and are extremely drafty. My mom stuffs the spaces between the windows and the frames with newspaper to make them a bit more airtight. In winter, I sleep in an army surplus sleeping bag in my bed with a mountain of blankets on top to keep me warm. None of this concerns me at all. I have my own room and I'm ecstatic.

Skeletons, Snakes, and Rats

Across from my school, and next to Mrs. Ashley's store, is a cemetery that is more than a hundred years old. The headstones are thin, barely legible, and many have been broken or toppled over. No one cares for the cemetery and it's overgrown with high grass and weeds. It's a perfect place to play soldier and war games after school. I don't play war games but discover that by pushing over headstones, I will find snakes and other critters. I capture two snakes and keep them in an aquarium in my basement.

When I'm in sixth grade, the Catholic Church buys the cemetery and removes human remains from the graves by using a big steam shovel. This disturbance causes hundreds of rats, that live in the cemetery, to scramble ahead of the steam shovel trying to find new homes. The streets around the cemetery are overrun with big rats who've fed well in there. It's scary to walk near the cemetery at night.

After school, I often stand by the cemetery fence next to Mrs. Ashley's and watch the steam shovel dig up graves. The bucket comes up from the graves full of dirt, broken parts of wooden coffins, human bones, and pieces of black clothing from tuxedos and funeral dresses. I find it interesting watching skulls and bones being sifted from piles made by the steam shovel and placed in wooden boxes. I'm told that the human remains will be re-buried at some other location owned by the Catholic Church.

Kids who play war games now use the opened graves for foxholes and strategically attack each other's foxholes yelling, "Geronimo", when jumping into the graves to fight the enemy.

When the graves have all been excavated and the last human remains removed, they're filled in and the ground leveled until construction begins. The site becomes an impromptu baseball field for afterschool games.

After I've left Francis Read and started at St. Nicholas, construction begins on what will become Saint Maria Goretti High School for girls. I hope the girls treat Mrs. Ashley with respect.

Dad Doesn't Die

My father gets tuberculosis as a teenager and isn't expected to live to twenty as there is no known cure. He does however make it to twenty, marry my mom, and have two kids, but spends months at a time at Eagleville Sanitarium for "treatment" of TB. The treatment consists of putting patients, wrapped in blankets, outdoors on army cots. Many of the patients get pneumonia and die from the cold. By his third or fourth residency at Eagleville, Dad has a collapsed lung, is coughing up blood, and isn't expected to make it out.

An intern not much older than Dad approaches him when he's on a cot outdoors. He tells Dad that he doesn't have much chance of surviving the winter and asks if he's willing to participate in trials of a new drug to treat TB. Figuring he has nothing to lose, Dad agrees. That drug proves to be the first treatment for TB that produces positive results. Dad's condition slowly improves and that young intern, Harry Beloff, becomes his friend and primary treatment doctor for the rest of his life. Dr. Beloff will go on to become head of Pneumology at Jefferson Hospital in Philadelphia and is considered one of the most knowledgeable and prominent experts on tuberculosis treatments in the country.

Dad continues to improve and eventually gets a job as a clerk in a meat-packing plant, then drives a cab for a while, and eventually passes a test for a clerical job with the Sanitation Department for the City of Philadelphia. He has to pass a physical and fearing the worst, he has his brother show up for the physical posing as him. He also lies about having a high school diploma. Sick with TB during his last year, he dropped out and never finished high school. He gets the job and is keeping books at an office in a stable where Sanitation Department wagons and horses are kept. He comes home nights, smelling of horses and wet dogs but he's able to keep the job without relapsing and that's good.

Just Second Class

There are four levels of advancement in Cub Scouts: Wolf, Bear, Lion, and Webelos. I join Cub Scout Pack 248, sponsored by St. Nicholas Church. My uncle Nick's best bud, Willie's wife, is our pack master. I stay with the Cub Scouts for several years only reaching the second level as a Bear.

I move up to Boy Scout Troop 248, and Willie is my Scout Master. Levels of advancement in Boy Scouts are more numerous and complicated. I never really apply myself and only reach Second Class in my Boy Scout career.

The only camping trip I ever participate in is at Breyer Training Area in Jenkintown, PA. Packing up my WWII surplus camping equipment in an army backpack, I board a bus in front of St. Nick's along with the other scouts. Arriving at the campground, we're instructed to pitch our pup tents facing downhill on a slight grade and dig a six-inch deep trough in a horseshoe shape around the tent to allow rainwater to pass without entering the tent. After hours of digging the trough and pitching the tent, I lay out my sleeping bag and blanket and unpack my cooking gear, looking forward to a late lunch.

A camp counselor with a foreign accent, instructs us on building a fire for cooking. We gather around to watch and learn. He assembles a pile of leaves, brush, and twigs, strikes a match and lights it up. The fire starts quickly assisted by a stiff wind but quickly spreads across the grass and into the woods. Our counselor panics and starts screaming in his strange accent, "CANTEEN, BUCKET, CANTEEN, BUCKET", as the fire increases in intensity and spreads. He begins shouting, "PICK UP TENT AND RUN. PICK UP TENT AND RUN." We promptly do, boarding our buses, leaving lots of equipment behind, and head for home.

When I tell my parents what happened, they decide that I won't be going on any more camping trips with Troop 248.

Heading into puberty suddenly makes scouting seem like kid stuff. I've reached Second Class, having only one Merit Badge in Reptile Study. Fortunately, no one finds out that my Garter and Eastern Coachwhip snakes escaped the aquarium in the cellar. I still haven't found them and probably never will. For months I have nightmares of being attacked by two large snakes in the cellar. I keep hoping that the rats eat them.

Somerdale: 1943-1953

Not Summer Camp

In 1941, the year I'm born, my father's parents buy an abandoned bungalow that's currently housing a neighbor's goats. It's in Somerdale, a very rural area of New Jersey, about twenty miles from South Philly. There's a paved road in front of the place with no sidewalk but most other roads in the town are dirt or sand. My grandfather's cousin Sam lives nearby and tips him off to the bargain property that will make a cheap summer home.

 Everyone in our extended family and many of our Camac Street friends and neighbors work on the bungalow on weekends for several years until it becomes a livable summer house.

Grandmom buys new furniture and household goods for their home in South Philly and furnishes the bungalow with the old furniture and household items plus donations from family and friends. Everyone who works on rebuilding the bungalow, or contributes in any way, is a welcomed guest at any time, forever.

During the earlier depression era, it was not uncommon for folks of limited means to fashion bed sheets, curtains, and even clothing from empty 50-lb cotton flour sacks, discarded by local groceries. Grandmom still uses these old depression-era handmade sheets for bedding, to the delight of neighbors who make fun of her, when she hangs them out still faintly bearing the "Gold Medal" flour logo.

By 1943, the bungalow is livable and Grandmom begins spending summers in Somerdale. With no one to keep an eye on us in Philly, there's no day camp or sleep-away for us. My sister and I are shipped off to spend summers with Grandmom.

For inner-city kids living in a grey world of coal-fired pollution, horse-drawn trash, milk, and coal wagons, spending summers in glorious sunshine and fresh country air, with endless fields and woods to roam, is nothing short of a miracle.

Our "summer camp" is this unheated bungalow with an icebox, no hot water, and a cesspool in the middle of the garden for fertilizer. Over the kitchen table, hanging from the ceiling, are flycatchers with three-foot-long brown sticky tape pulled from a small, hanging cylinder at the end that weighs it down. Flies land on and stick to the tape. Grandmom changes the flycatchers every few days when the tape is filled with dead flies.

Our bedrooms have no fans and only screens for ventilation. On weekends, when Grandpop is home, he goes around to all the open windows at night and sprays them from outside with a hand-pumped spray gun full of Black Flag DDT to keep mosquitos away. It's later discovered to be a deadly poison, but protecting us from mosquitoes is Grandpop's only concern now.

Each morning, Doris and I (she's four, I'm two) stand naked in front of the kitchen sink, shivering while

Grandmom scrubs us down with a washcloth of cold water and Octagon laundry soap. Saturday nights are bath nights, where large pasta pots are filled with water and put on the stove until boiling. They're poured into the bathtub that's plugged with a rubber stopper. My sister bathes first followed by me, in the same bathwater. It's barely warm by the time it's my turn but it still feels good.

Polio Boy

On hot summer days, we take turns sitting in Grandmom's large laundry washtub filled with cold water to cool off. We also chase each other with the garden hose, laughing and screaming with chilled delight, while being sprayed with cold water. It's the day after one of these afternoon "pool parties" that I wake changed forever.

In the summer of 1946, just weeks before my fifth birthday, I wake up to the sound of my family having breakfast in the kitchen. I get out of bed and fall. It feels like my right leg is "asleep". I rub it and try to wake it up and end the tingling burning sensation. I stand again and fall. I start crying and yell for my mom.

I'm in a hospital in a dark room laying on my stomach on a cold metal table with a single bright light above the table. My father's cousins, Nancy and Rosalie, are nurses here and they're called down to hold my hands while the doctor does a spinal tap. The pain is excruciating. It's determined that I have polio and must remain in quarantine in this hospital in the children's polio ward until the state deems me safe enough to return to my home and family in Philadelphia.

The boy's Polio Ward is a long, large room with about forty white, metal beds along both windowed walls and a row of beds in the center of the ward. Alone and without any family for the first time, I'm terrified, cry a lot, and want my mother to take me home. All the other kids cry a lot too.

One day a parent comes to visit her son and brings along a large bag of toys. She spreads them out on his bed and they play with them together until she leaves. He gets very upset, starts crying, and pushes all the toys from his bed onto the floor.

His bed is in the middle of the center row in the ward. All of us were able to watch him and his mother playing, wishing someone would bring us toys. With the toys now on the floor, we all struggle out of our beds, stumbling or crawling on the floor toward the toys, while crying in pain. Nurses hear the ruckus and come in to find a horrifying scene of crying crippled kids trying desperately to get to the toys. They pick up the toys, remove them from the ward, and put us all back in our beds. The crying and sobbing continue all afternoon. We never see the toys again.

I spend hours every day staring out the window by my bed, hoping to see Mom walking up the long sidewalk from the street. Several days a week after work, she takes a trolley from Philadelphia to Camden, NJ, and walks to the hospital to visit me. When she leaves, I always cry and beg her to take me with her. After three months, I'm released and allowed to return home to Camac Street for Thanksgiving with my family.

No one knows what causes polio or the epidemic that sweeps across the nation every summer. There is no known treatment or cure. I return to the hospital in Camden once a week for electric shock treatments to my right leg. They are painful and frightening but it's the only treatment for polio. Over several years, I gradually regain the ability to walk, have a slight limp and eventually live an almost normal life without many residual effects from polio. I'm very lucky. It won't be until 1955 that a vaccine is available that ends the annual epidemic, virtually eliminating polio in the United States and eventually most of the world.

POLIO PATIENTS USING PRIVATE SWIM POOL

Children from private homes who are under the care of the Philadelp Chapter, National Foundation of Infantile Paralysis, enjoying the pool at the G Knoll estate of Morgan Thomas, Moreland rd., Bethayres, Pa. yesterday. M Richard Bennett, left, head of State organization, is holding Patricia Gentile, 5, 2322 S. Rosewood st. Mrs. Jeanne Beck, chairman Polio Parents Club, and Morg Thomas, owner of estate, are with Edward Morgan 8, of 2124 E. Lehigh ave.

My first public appearance is in The Philadelphia Inquirer

Chickens

Grandmom gives me a quarter and I ride my bike a mile down Warwick Road to Mrs. Tamashek's house to buy a chicken. Mrs. Tamashek ties the feet of the live chicken together and stuffs it in the basket on my bike after collecting the quarter.

When I return, I give the chicken to Grandmom. She grabs it by the neck and pinwheels it 'til the neck snaps, slits its throat with a kitchen knife, then hangs it upside down on a garden pole until it bleeds out. We douse it in boiling water to soften up the feathers for plucking. Chicken feathers soaked in boiling water give off an unforgettable sickening stench, outdone only by the smell of singeing the remaining feather stubs over the stove. Grandmom guts it, saving the heart and some other innards for making soup later. She never roasts or fries chicken, but boils it with the skin still on and we're expected to eat it. It's smelly and slimy. Whenever I see chicken being served anywhere, I have boiled-chicken flashbacks.

The Victrola - His Master's Voice

A large, old hand-cranked Victrola sits in our living room, a relic of the 20s from my grandparents' house on Mifflin Street. There are shelves on the lower half of the Victrola that hold record albums of old 78s of Sicilian folk music, Sicilian comedy, and Italian favorites. You can adjust the volume on the Victrola by opening or closing the two doors covering the speaker horn. The needle is replaced after every record play. When you lift the lid to play records, there's a decal of a dog that appears to be listening to a large speaker horn with the words above it, "RCA Victor – His Master's Voice."

I love cranking up the old machine, putting in a needle, playing a record, and waiting for Grandmom to show up and start singing. She always tells the story that, when she was eight years old, the Pastor of the Cathedral in Caccamo, Sicily where she lived, asked her to sing solo and acapella at church services. She still has a beautiful voice and sings along loud and strong to the records I play. I become familiar with and love the music and songs of Sicily because of Grandmom's beautiful voice, even though I don't understand the words.

We have a series of comedy records, all featuring a Sicilian character name Donofrio. His misadventures with Americanized Sicilians express the frustration felt by newly-arrived Sicilians. Donofrio learns English very badly from a fellow immigrant. Donofrio learns to drive very badly from a fellow immigrant, etc. Grandmom translates the records for me as I play them but I don't think they're funny. I feel sorry for Donofrio. He's taken advantage of all the time by his own people.

Abbondanza

At the bungalow, we have no shortage of freshly-grown vegetables and beautiful flowers. As soon as the major rebuilding of the bungalow is completed, Grandmom promptly begins digging two-foot-wide flower gardens around the sides of the house. She also makes a large flower garden along the property. She loves having her hands in the dirt and plants as many flowers as she can, as fast as she can.

She gives my sister and me one zinnia seed each, shows us where to plant them, and tells us that we're responsible to see that our flowers grow tall and bloom beautifully. She shows us how to mix coffee grinds and crushed eggshells in the dirt around our flowers to make them grow big and strong. They do. My sister and I check on our flowers every morning to see if they need watering, how much they've grown and search for flower buds. Grandmom watches from the kitchen screen door and smiles proudly at us. I love watching my flower grow and hope someday to have my own flower garden.

About four feet from the road, Grandpop builds a rose arbor in front of the house and paints it white. He makes two small white benches inside. Grandmom plants climbing  roses that engulf the arbor and make it a beautiful romantic hideaway, except bees seem to love it too, so no one sits inside.

Grandpop digs a large garden for growing vegetables about twenty feet behind the house where the cesspool is located. It provides needed nutrients to the soil for good plant growth. He grows lettuce, string beans, squash, cabbage, beets, strawberries, and Jersey tomatoes the size of grapefruits.

He takes four peach pits and has my sister and I plant them ten feet apart on the edge of the garden closest to the house. The pits grow into trees as we grow. They never bear edible quality peaches but offer beautiful flowers in Spring.

The house has an uncovered back porch with two steps leading down to a large concrete patio. Grandpop builds a grape arbor along two sides and atop the patio. On hot summer evenings, we dine outdoors on the patio in the arbor, and in late summer we have lots of delicious, giant, concord grapes.

Farmer Dobbs

When we're low on milk, Grandmom gives me a dime and I ride my bike up the road to the Dobbs Farm. We don't know his first name and never call him Mr. Dobbs, just Farmer Dobbs. His son, Aaron, lost an arm in a tractor accident when young. He still works the farm on the tractor but is a loner, never sociable or friendly to me or anyone else.

Farmer Dobbs is in the barn mornings milking the cows by hand and occasionally shoots a stream of milk from a teat to one of the barn cats, who wait patiently for the treat. Farmer Dobbs takes the bucket of milk and pours it over a metal chiller. We then walk up to the house and Mrs. Dobbs fills a quart bottle with the chilled milk and seals it with a cardboard lid. By the time I get home, there's a thick mass of pure cream at the top of the bottle. If Grandmom isn't baking that day she'll let us drink the chilled cream. It's heaven in a bottle.

When I'm a bit older, Farmer Dobbs allows me and several other neighborhood kids to bring the cows back to the barn for the afternoon milking around four o'clock. We run through the fields and splash through creeks, following the sound of the cowbells while trying not to step in any freshly-made cowpies that litter the fields. We herd up the cows and bring them into the barn and do it for nothing, but a thank you. It doesn't seem like work to us. It's lots of fun.

Lazy Summer Days

I often go to ponds and lakes in the woods to collect tadpoles that I store in big pickle jars with pond water and duckweed. Watching them grow legs and feet, and gradually become small frogs, is amazing. I release them back in the pond when they're too big for the pickle jars.

For my birthday, I get my first fishing rod from the Sears

My 6th birthday party 1947 in Somerdale with family and friends. I'm not in the picture.

catalog. It's not a wooden rod, but one of the new, high-tech fiberglass ones. Mine has a very cool pistol grip with black plastic handles and a baitcasting reel.

51

My friend, Donnie, and I practice casting our fishing lines by putting a basket about twenty feet down the lawn and trying to land our weighted lines in the basket. We're eventually pretty good. We go fishing by an old mill near Laurel Springs, where we catch catfish, sunfish, and pike. Donnie gets to take them home 'cause the only fish Grandmom will cook and eat is bacalao. It's dried cod, preserved with salt, and has to soak in water overnight to make it soft enough to cook. I hate bacalao and promise myself that I will never eat bacalao when I'm a grown-up.

There's a large farm about a mile from my house that boards horses. Donnie is an expert rider and horse lover. On a beautiful sunny day, I accompany him to the farm, carrying a bag of apples and some clothesline. When we get to the fence at the edge of the field where the horses are grazing, Donnie takes the clothesline and ties it into a primitive halter. We take apples from the bag, wave them overhead, and whistle at the horses. Two eventually trot to the fence for the apples. As one horse is chewing an apple in my hand, Donnie climbs to the top rail of the fence, throws the halter over the horse's head, and jumps on the horse's back. Holding the halter and the horse's mane, he takes off and rides the fields for several minutes. returning with a big smile and a loud whoop. Donnie is the boy turned cowboy that I dream of being.

Wannabe Cowboy

Nothing is more exciting than taking a bus to Haddon Heights for Saturday afternoon movie serials with Roy Rogers or a John Ford Western like "She Wore a Yellow Ribbon." No adults; just me, my sister, and my two cousins. On the bus ride back home, my head is filled with images of me riding Trigger and shooting at bad guys or being in the cavalry and riding off to protect homesteaders. In my heart, I'll always be a cowboy and live by The Cowboy Code.

Clementon Lake Park

My Grandmother's sister Jenny ran the parking lot at Clementon Amusement Park for many years. We often get in for free, catch a bus on the corner and spend a day swimming and riding all the amusements. My favorite is the Roller Coaster, which I ride repeatedly, sitting in the first car with my arms held high in the air to show "looky-loos" that I'm not scared. I also love the Whip and the Bumper Cars. The Salt & Pepper Shaker looks so scary to me that I'll never get on for a ride but my sister and cousins

love it. The coolest is the Speedboat Ride in a beautiful mahogany Chris Craft.

The Park has a big 4th of July celebration every year that ends with fireworks. Everyone standing together in the center of the park watching the show gets showered with falling sparks and paper shards from the exploding fireworks. The sparks burn when they land on my skin.

Hayrides

A weekend treat that everyone loves is hayrides on horse-drawn old hay wagons with wooden-spoked wheels and red glass lanterns hanging off the back for tail lights. Teenagers on hayrides will often be smooching in the dark. We make fun of them and throw hay at them when they're kissing. Kissing a girl seems like such a dumb thing when you're eight years old.

The Northwestern School of Taxidermy

As a preteen, I'm an avid reader of outdoor fishing and hunting magazines. On the back pages of every magazine are advertisements for products and services. The Northwestern School of Taxidermy advertises in every magazine I read, promising to teach you how to mount that grizzly, ten-point buck, or buffalo head above your fireplace. I am captivated and want to be that guy with the grizzly bear head on his fireplace wall when I grow up.

I convince my friend Donny to chip in to purchase the at-home course from the school. While we're waiting for the course to arrive, we decide that we'll take the first steps on our own by killing and practicing taxidermy on

a bird. Donnie has a Red Ryder lever-action BB Rifle and, in his backyard, we hear the song of a yellow finch, or wild canary as we call them. We stalk the bird to a large willow tree in back of the garage and spot it on a low branch. Donnie lines up and sights the bird and takes a shot. The bird falls to the ground and we rush up to retrieve it. It's not dead. It's flapping around and can't fly or walk. Donnie and I are mortified. The bird is alive. There's very little blood. What do we do now? An unspoken decision is made to save this bird. We get a small box from the garage, line it with shredded newspaper, and place the wounded bird in it. We try feeding it and putting drops of water in its mouth but after several hours the bird dies. A chilling moment.

We dig a grave behind the garage, bury the bird, and leave bearing a terrible burden of guilt. Donnie and I never speak of this incident again but when The Northwestern School of Taxidermy instruction book arrives, I promptly toss it in the trash with the realization that I am not a born hunter and may never have an animal head on my fireplace wall.

Road Kill

I'm twelve years old, riding my bike down Warwick Road to Mrs. Tamashek's house to buy a chicken. I see a hunched-over person kneeling along the side of the road and stop to see if I can help. I'm disgusted to find a boy about my age skinning a dead raccoon that is apparently roadkill. I'm transfixed and feel nauseous at the same time. I ask him why he's doing that and he looks at me with a sneer. I ask if he lives around here and he points his knife toward a small house not far from Mrs. Tamashek's. I watch as he finishes skinning the raccoon, stands, and starts walking down the road with the wet raccoon pelt slung over his shoulder. I walk my bike alongside, tell him my name, and ask his. He says his name is Jerry.

That's how Jerry and I meet and become friends. He's from Romania, tall and thin for his age, with a very dark complexion. I learn that during WWII, he and his mother avoid starvation by killing and eating rabbits, squirrels, foxes, and even feral cats and dogs. His father is killed in the war and he and his mother come to America after the war. She works at a hospital in Camden as a nurse's aide. The only memories they took from Romania are a collection of hand-painted Easter eggs, an Eastern European tradition, now displayed in a dining room cabinet. My grandmother says they're gypsies and doesn't like them.

Jerry shows me his collection of roadkill pelts and the gloves, jackets, and trinkets he makes from the skins and the teeth he collects and makes into bracelets and necklaces. Gruesome for sure but I'm impressed. He's pretty cool. He's the same age as me but seems so much more mature and worldly. I'm gonna learn from this guy.

Jerry's mom always seems to be working so he's pretty much on his own. He tells me she smokes Kent cigarettes with "the Micronite Filter." He steals two cigarettes from the dining-room cabinet one afternoon and we take them into the woods across from his house. Several hundred yards into the woods, we come across a dirty, broken mattress lying in an opening in a cleared area. Jerry says that kids come here to have sex. I don't know what he's talking about or what that means but he picks up a dirty used condom, turns it upside down and gooey slime drips out. Eeewwww. He laughs and says they're dead babies. I have no idea what he's talking about. This kid is nuts.

He invites me to sit down on the mattress. He breaks out the two cigarettes, tears off the filters, and offers me one. I take it and we light up. He tries to show me how to inhale the smoke but I just end up coughing and eventually throw the cigarette away. Less than a year later, I'm proudly smoking unfiltered Chesterfield Kings and think I'm really cool.

The Berlin Farmers Market and Auction

Every Saturday night our entire family, and almost everybody in Somerdale goes to the Berlin Farmer's Market and Auction. My father, when he isn't hospitalized, always spends most of his time at the auction bidding on war-surplus stuff. He buys me a WWII folding paratrooper bicycle and used army equipment for Boy Scout camping. He also loves the used magazine stands. I think he's sneaking peeks at the girlie magazines.

I love the hawkers and hucksters who sell "miracle" car polish, used jukebox records, "incredible" arthritis cures, fortune tellers, raw clams on the half shell, and corn on the cob, dipped in butter on a stick.

I always pet the animals up for auction and don't realize what their fate will be until, one year, my uncle Leon buys a lamb at the auction and tethers it behind my grandmother's house. We love that lamb and make it our pet until we see Uncle Leon preparing to butcher it for Easter dinner. We cry and scream so much Grandmom orders him to take the lamb back to the auction and sell it. He was not happy that Easter.

Visitors

I always look forward to the arrival of the Iceman. He lays a thick piece of canvas over his shoulder and hoists up a big block of ice, using a large set of tongs. While he's carrying the heavy block of ice into the kitchen to load into the icebox, I hop up on the back of the truck and steal a few small, broken chunks of ice to suck on in the hot sun of summer.

The Freihofer Man stops by with his truck twice a week and Grandmom always buys fresh bread and treats for us. My favorite is glazed donuts. The sugar glaze sticks to my fingers and I lick them all clean.

Gypsies stop by regularly and try to sell us wooden lawn furniture they make. Grandmom makes us hide in the house whenever they come. She says gypsies kidnap kids and sell them to farmers who need workers. We believe Grandmom and we're afraid of the gypsies.

My parents come up on Fridays for the weekend and my grandfather and uncle Nick arrive on Saturday after closing the grocery store in Philly. I share a bedroom with uncle Nick and my sister sleeps on a cot in my parent's bedroom. We have large family dinners that also include my uncle Leon, aunt Marie, and their two kids, Leonard and Marianne, who live just down the road a bit.

Friends and neighbors from Camac Street often visit on weekends and help with lawn mowing, gardening, and other chores. It's fun for them and a chance to get out of the city for a bit. They leave well-fed, carrying bags of vegetables from the garden.

My favorite visitors are my grandmother's brothers and sisters, especially her brother, Joe. Uncle Joe always arrives with a gallon of wine, a set of bocce balls, and a guitar. You can bet there'll be lots of laughing, dancing, singing, bocce, and great family dinners.

Sweet Dreams

There's a metal glider on the front porch of our bungalow. My favorite memories of summers at Grandmom's are the lazy summer afternoons I lie on the glider rocking back and forth, falling asleep to the sound of cicadas and songbirds.

Left to right: Me, my cousin Lenny, cousin Bobby, my sister Doris, and cousin Marianne outside the tool shed. The tool shed was our playhouse. Somerdale around 1948, give or take a year.

Uncle Leon

Pre-Brando

In my neighborhood in South Philly, it's considered a mixed marriage when a person marries somebody from anywhere other than Sicily. My father's sister, Marie, marries a young stonemason from Central Italy named Leon.

Who could resist this guy? It's the middle of the Great Depression; he's all muscled up and looks like Charles Atlas. He commutes to NYC on a motorcycle several days a week to do stonework on the George Washington bridge for The WPA (The Works Progress Administration). He's makin' a hundred-and-twenty-five-bucks a week. This guy has to be "King of The Hill," right? Actually, no. He is resented by friends and neighbors who are hopelessly poor and unlike him, have few options.

He makes no attempts at all at being humble. In fact, he loves to flaunt his toys. He has a flashy car, a motorcycle, chain-smokes Lucky Strikes, and loves to show off his muscles and tan, wearing mostly "wife beater" t-shirts, which we call "Italian tuxedos." My uncle is my hero.

When the depression ends, Uncle Leon moves his family to South Jersey, near my grandmother's house. He works building mausoleums for rich people. Our family outings become Sunday picnics at his latest mausoleum project in cemeteries around the Philadelphia area.

Every day after work, he fills the trunk of his '39 Dodge with leftover chunks of granite. He stacks them neatly in piles on a new four-acre plot of land he buys across the street from my grandmother's house.

He also keeps a stash of smaller pieces of granite, on the floor of the passenger side of the Dodge. He doesn't believe in paying tolls, and says, "Roads are free," so when the automated toll machines are installed at the Ben Franklin bridge he speeds through and throws a chunk of granite in the machine. (This is before cameras are installed because he does this for years and is never caught.)

Over the next several years he slowly builds a home for his family with the entire facade of the house made of granite and stucco. This house is not only still standing, but it can probably survive a nuclear blast.

The Big Apple

Uncle Leon lives just across the road from Grandmom's house. He becomes my image of everything I think a man should be: a tough, strong, handsome, chain-smokin', wine-drinkin' stonemason, who hunts rabbits, pheasants, ducks, crows, and deer, and loves to fire his pistol and his shotgun in the air on holidays just for fun… and he spoils us kids rotten.

No one in our family drinks more than a glass of wine with dinner but Uncle Leon always keeps the gallon of wine alongside his chair during family dinners and refills his glass whenever he feels it's necessary. The more wine he drinks, the louder he talks and laughs. My grandparents glare but say nothing.

Some Saturday nights, Uncle Leon takes Aunt Marie for cocktails and dancing at The Big Apple, a small-town nightclub with NYC aspirations. At Sunday morning breakfast, Uncle Leon entertains us by pulling out a handful of Big Apple plastic swizzle sticks, heating them slowly at the center with his Zippo lighter, and folding them in half. They are now necktie clips with The Big Apple showing bright white against a red plastic background. He offers one to each of the men and boys in the family but no one seems excited about them, except me.

Charlie's Log Cabin Inn

On a blisteringly hot August afternoon, I'm out on the back lawn watching as Uncle Leon removes the washboard from Grandmom's large metal, washtub. He places it carefully against a post on the side of the back porch. He lifts one side of the large tub and tips it over. A wave of soap and bleach water foams out across the lawn and slowly soaks into the ground. I watch and wait.

Moments later, big, fat nightcrawlers start popping up through the grass and suds, like magic. I grab 'em and stash 'em in a Maxwell House coffee can. I spread a little dirt on them, cover it with wax paper, put a rubber band around the wax paper, and poke a fork through it, leaving four tiny holes for air. Uncle Leon smiles and nods, knowing he taught me well. I stash the can in the shade under the porch to save 'em, for when I go fishing.

He takes my hand, walks me across the lawn, and down the side of the road about twenty yards. We pass our neighbor's house, Charlie the Goat Man. We cross over the blacktop, and head down a narrow dirt road, passing Chicken Yocci's house; he's the weird neighbor that all the kids are afraid of. I push in close to Uncle Leon's leg and hold his hand tight, as we pass, hoping Chicken Yocci won't put the *Maloccio* on me.

We cut through an opening in a split-rail fence, encircling a lawn, with a long, low, log cabin in the center. There are old wagon wheels propped up with sticks on the lawn. It looks like a stagecoach stop in a John Wayne western movie. As we get closer to the cabin door, a small neon sign flashes *Charlie's Log Cabin Inn.* Uncle Leon pushes open the heavy, wooden door. I'm wild with excitement and have no idea that I'm about to fall down the rabbit hole forever.

The darkness blinds me for a moment, but I feel the cool air of the room on my cheeks. There's the smell of cigarette smoke, ashtrays, beer, and peanuts. I hear a Phillies game on the radio. Eddie Waitkus is on second, Richie Ashburn hits a homer and ties up the game.

As my eyes slowly adjust, I can make out a dim light over a circular bar in a large, open room with hot beams of intense sunlight shooting across the floor from tiny windows. There are some booths in the back, a jukebox, shuffleboard, a cigarette machine by the door, and a pinball machine against the front wall. It's an old Gottlieb machine with Lil' Abner and Daisy Mae painted on the glass. Daisy May is wearin' a really low-cut, tight-fittin' blouse.

Uncle Leon picks me up, sits me up on the bar, and pulls up a stool. He orders a coke for me and a beer for himself. He winks at me and we share the knowing smiles of two pals on a "road trip." He pops a stick match with his fingernail, lights up, and takes a long, slow draw on a Lucky Strike, while the barkeep draws his beer. The bartender yells over, "Hey kid, what's your name?" I softly answer, "Phillip". He comes back from the register, hands Uncle Leon the beer, and offers me a handful of nickels painted with red nail polish. "Ever play pinball, Phillip?" My face lights up like a neon sign. I nod a silent, "Yeah," yell a quick, "Thanks," and leap from the bar, one hand full of red nickels the other full of peanuts, arms pushed up high in the air. I make a mad dash for Daisy Mae wearin' a shit-eatin' grin, wider than the Grand Canyon. For me, this moment remains frozen in time forever. I know I'm home!

Life Lessons

Although he has no formal education other than apprenticing as a stonemason, Uncle Leon teaches me the Latin phrases for mass, so I can become an altar boy, and how to pee along the garden edge to keep animals away. He knows which mushrooms will poison you and which ones you can eat, how to catch catfish with just a string and a piece of bread, how to catch a bird using a cardboard box, a stick, a slice of bread, and some string. I learn that you can slice the tongue of a baby crow with a razor blade and teach it to talk like a parrot. What more could any seven-year-old possibly need to know about life!

Forever My Hero

After fifty years of breathing granite dust and chain-smoking three packs of Lucky Strikes a day, Uncle Leon's lungs slowly turn to stone and he spends his last years in a fragile state on oxygen until passing at seventy. In my mind, he is forever the heavily-muscled Charles Atlas in the comic ads, protecting us from bullies who would kick sand in our face on the beach.

Living in Two Worlds

On Being Christ-like

When my sister finishes sixth grade at Francis Read, she should be attending Furness Junior High School before advancing to South Philadelphia High School. Our parents decide there are too many black kids at Furness and feel she won't be safe there. They switch her to Catholic school at St. Nicholas, our parish church.

Two years later I'm in seventh grade at St. Nicholas, totally buying into being a good Catholic and possibly even a priest. I become an altar boy serving mass in Latin and Italian every morning at 8:30 AM. We actually get tips from parishioners for serving mass. All the altar boys pool tips, and at the end of the school year, the nuns take us on a trip to Washington, DC, funded by our tips.

I impress the nuns with my ability to easily diagram sentences but as a left-hander, I do not do well in penmanship having to use an ink-filled fountain pen. I smear the ink as I'm writing and fail penmanship. On the other hand, I'm being coached with extra assignments to prepare me for a possible scholarship to Saint Joseph Preparatory School. It's a prestigious learning institution that prepares smart Catholic boys for admittance to Villanova University, the dream of every Catholic parent with a son. Saint Joe's Prep is not to be.

On learning that I was Captain of the Safety Patrol at Francis Read, Mother Superior drafts me into their AAA Safety Patrol Program where I enter as Lieutenant. I'm charged with ensuring that students don't run in the halls or on the stairs and that there are no students in the halls after the class bells ring. My chest is swelled with pride and a feeling of importance and of doing a good job: Something that I apparently crave, 'cause of lacking my Dad's approval.

Why They Bombed Pearl Harbor

Our assignment is to write an essay on American history. I bravely write a biting and intensely honest autobiography citing my birth as a great moment in American history. I intimate that the Japanese were so shaken by my birth and how it might affect their future world domination plans that they bombed Pearl Harbor as a warning shot.

I read it aloud in class and there's lots of laughter from both my fellow students and Sister Grace, our teacher. Though others have done historical research for their essays, I

receive this, my first writing award, for a humorous take on history as I perceive it. This is the first inkling of my soon-to-be-emerging cynical sense of humor. It may not seem great compared to the Pulitzer Prize  but to a twelve-year-old in 1953, it makes my year.

Off to the Burbs

Following World War II, America is changing rapidly and dramatically with Levittown-type instant communities. The rural suburban areas surrounding Philadelphia are being heavily developed into new towns of row houses with lawns, garages, and wide streets. My parents, like many other working-class Italians, German, Irish, and Polish are eager to leave the city.

Dad continues to take advancement tests with the City and scores well enough to land a great job as a Senior Accounting Clerk in the City Treasurer's Office. That job, plus Mom working in a clothing factory as a seamstress, allows our family to slowly move up from being poor working-class to middle-class by the mid-fifties.

 In 1954 Mom and Dad buy a house in a subdivision of a development named Westbrook Park. Our new section is called Briarcliff and we move to a corner house on Stratford Road at Crescent Drive. Imagine how cool I feel telling the kids at my school in South Philly that I now live on Crescent Drive. In all of South Philly, there are no street names ending in "Drive." We are now officially middle-class.

Having to commute daily to work and school, we need a new family car. Dad's old '49 Kaiser-Frazer is replaced by a '52 Kaiser for the daily commute. The towns, in which these new developments are built, did nothing to prepare for the dramatically-increased population. This shortsightedness results in overcrowded schools, a lack of sufficient police and firefighters, and two-lane roads that are unable to handle the increased daily-commuting traffic. What was a five-minute walk to St. Nicholas is now a forty-five-minute-to-an-hour bumper-to-bumper traffic jam

68

going to and coming from the city. BUT WE HAVE A
LAWN AND A GARAGE.

Surprise

Our new development has no resources or identity other
than a small shopping area in the center. We're listed by the
Postal Service as living in Glenolden Township and are
assigned that town address and zip code. For still unknown
legal, political or social reasons, we are officially
designated a part of Darby Township, a black community
about five miles from our development. Thinking they left
the city and black people behind, Mom and Dad and a lot
of our white neighbors are surprised to find that we're now
policed and governed by black people. Ahhh, the irony!

Bad Boy

"Though the cowman might break every law of the territory, state, and federal government, he took pride in upholding his own unwritten code."

-Ramon F. Adams

Philly Mummer's Parade 1950s Style - Doing "The Mummer's Strut"

The Cedarwood Counts 1953-1959

I begin making friends with boys in my new neighborhood. Most are Italian-Americans from South Philly and we have a lot in common. My circle of friends eventually expands to include Irish and German-American boys who grew up across the road from our development: Jack, Butch, Donnie, Billy, Ralph, Buddy, Tommy, Pete, and Willie. We hang out at the Cedarwood Pharmacy, drink nickel fountain cokes, and I begin smoking in earnest, Chesterfield Kings. We're soon calling ourselves The Cedarwood Counts as all boys about to hit puberty wanna be in a "gang" and thought of as tough.

As a gang, the Cedarwood Counts will be 1 for 2 in gang fights. Our first is with tough kids from "the projects" who are around our age. We successfully defend our turf when they try to take over our corner at the Cedarwood Pharmacy. A week later, their older teenage brothers hunt us down in retribution and we get our asses kicked. That pretty much ends my career as a Cedarwood Count but I continue to pursue other options on the road to "badass."

After graduating from St. Nicholas, my parents enroll me in Saint James High School for Boys in Chester, PA. where my life is about to change dramatically. I begin puberty, get my first hard-on, and being a good Catholic quickly drops off my radar. It's replaced with the drive to find a girlfriend. This endeavor will prove futile while dealing with years of furious acne breakouts leaving me angry and depressed.

No Mere Mummers, We!

In the 50s, the Philadelphia Mummer's Parade on New Year's Day is not yet televised, is almost exclusively white, and does not allow women. It's a great time for rowdy teenagers to get drunk, try to pick up girls, and generally behave like assholes; I'm no exception. I get a pint of 100-proof cheap vodka from a wino at the bowling alley, dress up in my warmest, cool-lookin' threads, and head to Broad Street to join the chaos.

The marchers form below Snyder Avenue on Broad Street and the parade officially kicks off at Broad Street and Snyder Avenue in front of Southern High. They parade up Broad Street to City Hall where there's a grandstand with judges who determine the winners in each category: Comics, Fancy Division, and String Bands. The Comics satirize and make fun of everything and everyone, particularly politicians, with clever and often obscenely offensive displays and costumes. The Fancy Division wears glamorous plumed outfits and is judged on the quality and originality of their costumes and floats. The String Bands also wear plumed and decorative, original costumes and march while playing banjos, saxophones, drums, and other string instruments.

This sounds classy and impressive but many Mummers, particularly in the Comics Division, begin morning drinking before the start of the parade and some don't make it to City Hall for the judging. Several pass out drunk on the street and have to be carried off while other drunken Mummers randomly grab and kiss women watching the parade who seem startled at first but are generally agreeable.

There is only one openly gay, glamorously dressed, Drag Queen in the parade every year and he/she is only known as Francine the Queer by friends and haters alike. Francine the Queer is a tough Italian kid who loves to beat the shit out of anyone who dares to make fun of him.

After passing the judge's stand, they parade across Market Street to Second Street, called Two Street in South Philly. When they turn and march down Two Street, the real bacchanal begins, led by the great Polish American String Band. South Philly, from the Delaware River to Fourth Street, is mostly inhabited by Polish-Americans who love to party with the String Bands and other paraders. Wild partying continues well into the night.

My friends and I are patrolling the sidewalk on Broad Street from Snyder Avenue up to Morris Street by the Savoia Theater. We're grabbing and kissing girls, cursing, spitting on people, picking fights, getting drunker, louder, and more obnoxious as the day goes on. I go to the parade every year and repeat this same moronic behavior throughout my four years of high school. I think I'm a badass and cool as hell.

Tommy's Jeep

Tommy Grogan's a tough Irish kid two years older than me. He lives across Ashland Avenue in the old part of our town. He doesn't particularly like me or any of the new kids in the developments, but he's a Junior at St. James, has a 1950 Jeep pickup, and needs gas money.

Four or five of us "newbie" freshmen chip in a few bucks a week and Tommy lets us ride to school in the open back of the pickup. It's a one-way trip 'cause most of us hitchhike home after  school. Our parents give us money every week to ride the bus to and from school, but by riding with Tommy and hitching home, we have enough to buy cigarettes. A pretty cool arrangement that works for everybody.

One of our favorite fun things to do while riding to school is tossing firecrackers at the bus stops on McDade Blvd, where lots of guys and girls are waiting for buses. Suckers! Always a good laugh watching them scramble and yell curses at us.

Skating Squad Badasses

Students at St. James High School for Boys are mostly Irish-American and I'm welcomed by my fellow students with the nickname "Meatball." This results in the need to prove both my newly-emerging masculinity as well as my worthiness as a potential friend. Having just reached puberty, I eagerly engage in behavior that will lead to detentions.

I organize and lead a student strike against the school bookstore which is managed by my Latin teacher. Students are forced to buy textbooks for classes from the school-run bookstore at highly marked-up prices. Overcharging for these books is too nice a word. The strike lasts a week and eventually dies when most of the strikers and I, in particular, are threatened with suspension and given the option of detention if we end the strike. We accept. My activity during the strike has lasting consequences for my Latin teacher.

Not satisfied with the answers I'm offered in Religion class, I mimeograph and distribute to my class a daily newsletter, *The Roman Times*. It offers alternative facts for how Jesus managed to have himself declared the Messiah, prophesied in the Old Testament, and offers logical explanations on how he may have pulled off his alleged "miracles". This too has consequences for me at year's end.

As if that's not enough, I organize a student walk-out on a day when all public and Catholic schools in Delaware County, except our school, are closed during a heavy snowstorm. The walkout is successful and soon guarantees me a permanent spot on the dreaded Skating Squad.

There are three stages of detentions at St. James:

#1 *The Standard* study hall detention where students report to the auditorium after school, check in, and quietly read books or do homework for an hour before being released. Strictly for nerds and geeks.

#2 *The Crucifixion*. If the standard detention doesn't encourage you to change your errant ways, you are graduated to *The Crucifixion* detention, a stronger incentive for behavioral compliance. Crucifixion detentionees are made to kneel in the aisle of the auditorium with arms outstretched. A heavy book is placed in each hand. When arms tire and the books are dropped, the priest in charge whacks the back of your head with a book and replaces them in your outstretched hands. This is repeated for the entire hour and good detentionees bear silent witness to what will become their fate should they choose not to walk the straight and narrow. I wonder, "What would Jesus think?" of this mockery of his actual crucifixion.

My refusal to follow rules results in enough accumulated detentions to last through my remaining three years of high school. By mid-Sophomore year, I'm assigned to the most dreaded form of detention.

#3 *The Skating Squad.* Every Friday, instead of my regular *Crucifixion* detention, I now report to the school gym. Heavy towels are tied to my shoes and, along with the other Skating Squad miscreants, am made to polish the entire gym floor. We dip the towels in liquid wax and "skate" around the gym until the floor is waxed sufficiently to satisfy the impossibly-demanding requirements of the priest in charge. Depending on the number of students on the Skating Squad on any given week, it could take anywhere from an hour to two hours or more of extreme muscle-cramping-ice-skating-movements, leaving calves and thighs twitching painfully for hours afterward. Permanently assigned to the Skating Squad for the remainder of the school year, my determination to resist at all costs hardens as my legs gain strength and power.

The Skating Squad crew and I are looked upon by regular students as tough bad-asses, who buck the system and are not to be fucked with. Most of our classmates now want to be our friends. Achieving my end goal of becoming a respected, cool, badass, I'm content in my newly-proven masculinity. I strut down the halls like a proud peacock in my leather motorcycle jacket and boots, ala Brando in "The Wild One." I keep a bottle of cheap apple wine in a mouthwash bottle in my locker that I sip regularly between classes. I'm badder than bad.

When school ends in June, I've flunked Latin, Religion, and Algebra II. Failing Latin and Religion was in part the result of my bookstore strike and the anti-Catholic newsletter. I'm not surprised. Failing second-year Algebra only proves that I have no aptitude whatsoever for anything in mathematics past times tables. I'm required to go to summer school and receive passing grades if I want to return to St. James. I hunker down and take Latin and Algebra classes, barely passing both with a "D." I refuse to take the make-up Religion class 'cause it's bullshit. I'm not allowed back for my Junior year at St. James. My career in Catholic school ends, along with any remaining belief in Catholicism.

I'm thinkin' of myself now as a genuine juvenile delinquent. I prove it by getting arrested on Felony Breaking and Entering charges in July. I spend a night in jail, get a year's probation, lose my driver's license for a year, and am pretty much grounded by my parents... but I AM A BADASS now!

My Own Bible

Leaving Catholicism behind is natural and easy for me. From the 40s on I've been imbued with a code of ethics and morals learned on daily radio serials, later by western movies, and my addiction to western novels of Louis L'Amour and later, Larry McMurtry. The Cowboy Code of personal integrity and honor seems a believable moral

79

choice more than the hypocritical practices of most male Catholics I grew up around. They seem misogynistic and unaccepting of anyone who is not of their religion, ethnicity, or race. I cannot be that person. It may seem childish and naive to many but The Cowboy Code provides a better moral compass for my life than religion.

The Dance King

I'm fifteen. I get a job setting pins at Stony Creek bowling alley. I work League Nights and Saturdays and get $.11 a game, $.22 when I set double lanes. I ride to work on the back of my friend Donny's '48 Harley. On paydays, we chip in and give a couple bucks to an old wino who works with us to buy wine. He gets a gallon for himself and a gallon of Apple wine for us. We get drunk before every dance we go to on Friday nights.

I'm a really good fast dancer or what we call "Jitterbuggin'". I enter dance contests all over Delaware County and never lose. When you go to a dance contest outside your own neighborhood and win the contest, you get beat up by the locals for winning, unless you bring along protection. I always bring along guys from my neighborhood. I fill them up with apple wine and while everyone's standing in a circle watching the contest dancers, my guys go through the girls' purses left on the metal folding chairs along the wall and take their money. That's their "vig" for coverin' my ass. Hey, that's the life of "bad boys" now.

Ralph's Gym

My friend Ralph and his brother Buddy grew up in Glenolden and live in a single home with a large patio out front. They have a big basement, where Ralph and Buddy regularly work out with weights.

Ralph invites us to work out with him and four of us go for it. A few days a week, Louie, Paul, Pete, and I join Ralph and,  sometimes Buddy, for a workout in the basement. We begin calling it Ralph's Gym and start gettin' serious about building up muscle strength and definition. Ralph is soon nicknamed "Pecs", while I'm now known as "Lats", Louie is "Biceps", Pete is "Abs", and Paul, soon to be a champion shotput athlete at St. James, is called "Traps" for his prominent trapezius muscles. Ralph and Paul consider the possibility that Louie, Pete, and I may not be as serious or dedicated to fitness as they are. We're often doing curls, deadlifts, bench presses, and pushups with cigarettes dangling from our lips. Just tryin' to be cool while gettin' healthy.

Dave's Tombstone Tavern

At sixteen I have my first "sit down" beer with my seventeen-year-old buddy Jack in "Dave's" in Glenolden. It has the same smell and feel as Charlie's Log Cabin Inn. I'm wearing my dad's jacket to look older. I feel really grown up and try not to get drunk and embarrass myself. Jack and

I become regulars drinking draft beer after school a couple of days a week.

Easy Riders

Sam, the owner of the Cedarwood Pharmacy, owns an old grey junker he uses to deliver prescriptions. It's a '48 Plymouth Coupe, a salesman's model with a very large trunk and no back seat. The bench front seat can fit three comfortably. Sam leaves it parked in front of the pharmacy at night. He never bothers locking the car 'cause he can't imagine anyone would steal this junker.

Sam's old Plymouth has a three-post ignition. At fourteen, my sister's boyfriend, Johnny Boy, taught me how to short the three-post ignitions with silver foil from a cigarette pack. You just jam the silver foil in tight, making sure it's touching all three ignition posts. That done, you hit the starter button, it kicks over, and you're off like a cheap prom dress.

When Louie, Jack, and I get bored at night we swing by the pharmacy and hotwire the Plymouth. We drive up to McDade Boulevard, cruise down to Norwood, and check out the chicks. Once in a while, we throw a buck's worth of cheap Safeway gas in just so we don't feel too guilty about borrowing the car. Sam never seems to notice. We're never stopped or caught by the police.

The Wedding Crashers

My best friend Louie and I spend the Springs and early Summers of 1956 and '57 crashing wedding receptions on weekends. Most receptions are held in church basements and firehouse halls. Every weekend around 8:30 PM, we dress up in suits and ties and drive around Delaware County checking churches and firehouses for receptions. When we find one that looks good and there's a crowd out front smoking, we park, light up a cigarette, and casually saunter over to mingle in the crowd. While talking, we slowly work our way through the crowd and when we finish our cigarettes, we casually walk inside the reception hall, talking and laughing, as though we've been here all along.

The party's usually been going on for a few hours when we arrive so everyone's pretty relaxed and having a good time. Italian roast beef sandwiches are very popular at receptions so we grab a plate and a few sandwiches. We then head over to the bar for a Rolling Rock nip. That's pretty much the standard beer for receptions around here. No one gets carded at a wedding so we grab our beers and head for a couple of empty seats.

Reception halls usually have the bride and groom's families on separate sides of the room. We determine which family's side we're sitting on. If anyone asks who we are, we tell them our first names and say that we're with the other family and couldn't find a chair there. We ask if they mind if we finish our food. They're always very accommodating and friendly.

After eating and having a few beers, Louie and I go out for a smoke and when we return, we scout around for some good-looking chicks. We dance a few numbers with several different girls and use the same line if they ask which family we're with. Sometimes we even get lucky and get a phone number. We always leave before the cake-cutting ceremony, going out front for a smoke and sauntering our way back down to our car. We never get stopped or seriously questioned at any of the many receptions we crash over two years; we're that cool.

Not On the Wall of Fame

 Still living in Glenolden in September, using my grandparents' address in South Philly, I enter South Philadelphia High School, where I'm enrolled in the Academic curriculum. South Philadelphia High School is just called "Southern" in South Philly. The school has just been rebuilt, modernized, and air-conditioned with a large schoolyard and a student-smoking lounge outside the cafeteria.

Southern has a long list of famous alumni including opera singers Marian Anderson and Mario Lanza, actor Jack Klugman, singer Chubby Checker, singer Frankie Avalon, jazz musician Charles Earland, heartthrob Fabian Forte, and many more. I will never be joining them on The Wall of Fame outside the Principal's office.

Having grown up in an ethnically isolated neighborhood, I find that attending school now with Blacks, Jews, Irish, Polish, and other non-Sicilian Italians offers a preview of how the real world looks. I find that I'm perfectly comfortable with making new friends from other cultures and races. I love the freedom of Public School, where discipline takes a distant second place to actual learning. I thrive there with minimal studying and mostly try to stay as invisible as possible offering no reason for detentions.

My dad, mom, sister, and I had two of the same teachers in elementary school, Mrs. McDermott and Miss Porter. Now at Southern, I have two teachers that my father had classes with.

Mr. Nelson, my Physics teacher is still wearing the same three-piece navy-blue wool suit every day that he wore when my father was in his class. On the first day of roll call, Mr. Nelson asks if my father was the previous Giambri who had taken his class. When I nod yes, he says he remembers flunking him and will be keeping a sharp eye on me too. Having no gift for math or physics I barely squeak by and finish his class with a "D".

Our other shared teacher is the elegant and witty Mr. Paravicini, who also remembers my dad. I love his class, write some of my best high school assignments for him and finish with an A+. He, like Mrs. McDermont at Francis Read, also comments on my report card that I should pursue a writing career. How I manage to disregard these important cues for so many years only testifies to my chosen ignorance in all things academic!

I learn that instead of spending a boring hour in the auditorium reading or doing homework during Study Hall periods, I can volunteer as an Office Aide in the school's Main Office. The fox is inadvertently invited into the chicken coop. As an Office Aide, I discover the private filing cabinets containing blank report cards, elevator passes, and nurse's passes. BINGO! I am now able to doctor my report cards to mask from my parents the many days I hook school and pad my grades to make me seem uniformly brilliant. My parents are amazed at my dramatic turnaround from Catholic school behavior. I hook school at least once a week, leave classes at will with counterfeited Nurse's passes, and always ride elevators between classes. In addition to availing myself of these golden privileges, I also earn cigarette money by selling them to select friends.

South Philly, Here We Come Again!

All city employees are required to live in Philadelphia. Someone who, apparently, doesn't like my father, reports to the city that he's living in Glenolden. We either move back or he loses his job. There's a new development just finished in South Philly, very close to the Navy Yard. In the summer of 1958, my parents buy a house in Packer Park, where the streets are named for naval heroes. We live on Forrestal at 18th Street, just around the corner from the Packer Bar, a notorious hangout for rowdy Navy submariners.

High school yearbook photo
with a blurb that is mostly fiction, except for the Navy.

I'm in the second graduating class of the "new" Southern High, in June of

PHILLIP GIAMBRI
3221 S. Broad Street

"Flip," who is going to follow the Navy, loves fishing, dancing, and girls. Active in Stunt Nite, an S. A. representative, band, class chairman, and counselor's aide. Flip also played intramural basketball. Popular Flip has good reason to say, "School is the most!"

1959, with more than a thousand graduates. I'm handed an Academic diploma, have surprisingly good actual grades, and leave with the deep satisfaction of having triumphed over Catholic school detentions and administrative rule makers.

86

I will soon enter the US Navy in October of '59. Boot Camp presents monumental challenges for someone who doesn't follow rules well and has little respect for authority. Growing up does not come easy or early for me.

Ed Mack's Tavern

I finish high school at seventeen, turn eighteen in August, and am waiting to leave for the Navy in the fall. I work at Curtis Publishing Company loading books on and off their ancient electric trucks, with solid tires, whose top speed is 11mph.

Paperback books are the new craze and working at Curtis, I quickly build a library of all the great books that are being newly released in paperback. A gold mine for me.

My buddies and I have lunch every day at Ed Mack's Tavern around the corner. We soon discover that, even though we're all under twenty-one, the bartender, Harry, is willing to serve us alcohol. We quickly switch from cokes to beer for lunch and start hangin' out there at night after work. We're regularly getting drunk nights on rum and cokes.

Pasties and a G-string

My last day at Curtis Publishing Co. is followed by a farewell party after work, thrown by my co-workers. We start at Ed Mack's with Rum & Cokes and a burger, then head over to Chinatown for a show at The Troc. How could any eighteen-year-old virgin be expected to go off to the Navy and see the world without at least once having been to the infamous Troc!

 The Troc was once an opera house, then a vaudeville house, and, by the late fifties, it's degenerated into a "burlesque" house. In fact, it's more like a sleazy strip joint, where pervs and creepy old men jerk off in the front rows.

Tonight's featured performers are Torrine the Tassel Tosser, Meela the Peela, and Vera Flame. Now there's a million-dollar-Vegas lineup for ya!

We get the cheap seats in the balcony and watch these tired old ladies dry hump the curtain, tease the front row jerkoffs, and carefully strip away their garments, revealing somewhat less than perfect bodies. Vera Flame, the star of the show, is actually kinda hot. Saggy tits and all, she's still good enough to make this eighteen-year-old virgin's dick hard.

We end the night with a few more rounds of drinks at Ed Mack's and a sad goodbye. I'm off to the Navy with flashes of Vera Flame's breasts still fresh in my mind.

Salty Coffee

It's the late 50s, the height of the Cold War. I join the Navy and, after boot camp, I'm assigned to the USS Independence, an aircraft carrier operating out of Naples, Italy. I'm leading a miserable life, twelve decks below the water line, working in one of the four boiler rooms that provide steam to launch the fighter planes.

The backwoods boys in the boiler room hate anyone from any city and anyone with more than an elementary-school education. They are determined to break this "Pizza Face" Italian and his fellow "City Boy Jew". My Jewish friend eventually has a nervous breakdown and disappears from B Division. I'm gonna be next, the way they're workin' on me.

Against Navy and all safety regulations, they have me standing on top of a working 1,200-pound boiler, replacing asbestos lagging on the heat pipes above, without ever a thought of using a face mask. It's so hot that the soles on my boots melt. I'm given scores of extremely difficult, dirty, and, sometimes impossible tasks and timelines. I'm angry and getting' near my limit, but hangin' on. I have deep, dark fantasies of murdering these freakin' ridge-runnin' assholes in their sleep.

When I have to make coffee for these bastards, I piss in the coffee pot. They complain that I'm making the coffee with seawater. I don't reply and piss in the coffee pot at any opportunity.

Momma Never Told Me

We have liberty nights in ports along the Mediterranean coast during the six months I'm aboard the USS Independence. At my paygrade, I mostly drink grappa, the cheapest drink available everywhere, except for wine. In Greece, I attend a wine festival for next to nothing and drink all day for free. It's my first experience with alcohol poisoning. I'm puking green liver bile for a week and wish I were dead. I'm stickin' to grappa after that.

In 1960, despite the Olympics being held in Rome, much of Southern Italy and Sicily are still suffering the effects of massive American bombing during WWII. The filthy streets of Naples, our home port, are the territory of gangs of orphaned kids. They surround tourists and sailors like a swarm of bees, leaving you without hat, wallet, wristwatch, or cigarettes. Palermo in Sicily isn't any better. Desperately in need of repair, buildings along the waterfront still have their outside walls missing and have makeshift coverings, fashioned from army blankets.

With roving gangs of kids on the loose in Palermo, I always feel unsafe here and never consider trying to visit family in Caccamo, about an hour away. I can't imagine what might be going on there just waiting for an American sailor to come along.

There are public urinals on the streets of many Italian cities and it's surprising to me that men walking along just unzip at a urinal and do their business in public. I don't think of myself as a prude but I'm not ready for that yet. Not this Philly boy.

On the other side of the coin, on the French Riviera, I find in nightclubs and bars, men and women share the same bathroom with no booth or door separating them. For the first time in my life, I enter a bathroom to find myself staring at a woman on the toilet peeing with her legs spread. It is not easy to act nonchalant while blushing in bright, neon red.

There's also a nightclub with a live sex act between a woman and a donkey. I heard sailor stories about these sex acts in Tijuana but I never imagine seeing this in France.

Monaco seems home to the largest number of Rolls Royces and beautiful prostitutes in the world. Everything is too beautiful and too classy and too expensive here for a sailor making $89 a month.

On liberty in Barcelona, Spain, I buy a custom-made pair of riding boots, tan with red stitching, for a very reasonable price. I cherish these boots. The craftsmanship is beyond anything I could ever afford in Philadelphia.

Barcelona is a beautiful city but I find the women in bars to be extremely aggressive in soliciting sailors by getting you hard while negotiating price. My low, monthly pay puts me out of the range of most of these sexy salesladies, who touch while bargaining. It sure feels nice, though.

Drinkin' My Dolphins

Every week aboard ship, I put in a request for Submarine School, one of the few ways you can get transferred from a

91

carrier. I eventually get orders to Sub School in New London, CT. Upon completion, I'm assigned to one of the very first nuclear Polaris missile submarines, USS Patrick Henry.

We operate out of Holy Loch, Scotland, and regularly deploy off the coast of Russia on sixty-day patrols... just in case they decide to start World War III. We're part of a "Strategic Deterrent Force" and, in the event of a missile attack on the United States, we will retaliate by firing our missiles in a brilliantly cynical plan called *Mutually Assured Destruction*, or *MAD*. Ironic, huh? On my second Cold War Patrol, I complete a very intensive Submarine Qualification training program. When we return to Holy Loch, my buddies take me up to Glasgow, to the notorious Beresford Lounge, to be initiated into a very elite brotherhood of sailors entitled to wear the Submariners "Dolphins" insignia.

Out of respect for those with weak stomachs, I won't go into the details of the initiation ceremony, but I leave The Beresford totally shitfaced, along with my friend Gary, and two equally drunken hookers. On the way to their "hotel", we're chatting up the cab driver and convince him to stop and have a few drinks with us. The cabbie gets really drunk and Gary volunteers to drive the remaining couple of blocks to the whorehouse... I mean "hotel". He's had way too much to drink, and never drove on the other side of the street. We bounce our way down the street side-swiping about six cars before we get to the whore-house. We leave the cabbie laid out in the back seat of the cab, check into the hotel, and proceed to get it on.

Later, I'm relaxing in bed, while the "lady of the evening" is getting us more drinks. I decide to take a stroll downstairs through the lobby. No one seems to notice or care that I'm really drunk and very naked. Across the lobby, I spot a woman I recognize, pouring a glass of wine for some guy. I remember her from a nasty incident in a bar in Dunoon. I stagger toward her yelling, "Hey, you stole Mike's radio." She sees me, turns fast, breaks the wine bottle on the edge of a table, and charges, aiming the broken bottle directly at my face. She's cursing at me and laughing like hell as she chases me over the broken glass until I'm out of the lobby and making a mad dash for the stairs.

I find Gary's room, knock hard, yelling at the door, "Gary, I'm in trouble. We gotta' get outta' here, now!" The door opens and there's a huge erection staring up at me. The hooker's standing behind him smiling, wearing his open peacoat. Wow! She has nice boobs! He leans into my face and slurs out, "I ain't leavin' 'til I get laid... again!" "Gary, it's me, your best friend!" "You're on your own, pal!" He slams the door in my face.

I stagger back to my room, fumble into my uniform, and run barefoot down to the train station, carrying my shoes, my coat, and my hat. The last train to Dunoon already left and the station is closed for the night. I toss the night watchman a couple of bills and he lets me sleep on the empty morning train for the remainder of the night. The train suddenly starts moving and I wake up. For a second, I almost think I'm sober. I look down. My feet are all cut up, covered with dried blood, and burning like hell. My mouth tastes like ass, my head's exploding, and where in hell are my socks? I catch a glimpse of those shiny new Dolphins pinned to my uniform and break into a big-ass grin. "God Damn, I'm a real Submariner now!" Despite everything that's happened, this is gotta' be the proudest moment of my life.

To be, or Not to Be?

The Sub Base Players: Where it Begins

During four Cold War patrols and two years aboard, I'm
regularly writing comedy and fiction stories for our ship's
daily newspaper, *Silent Service Breakfast News*. Our
Weapons Officer also writes an anonymous daily
comedy/fiction column in the newspaper. He and I spend
many hours on watch discussing literature, writing, and my
future. He becomes my mentor and suggests that, instead of
spending my off-time in New London drinking all day, I
should think about doing something a bit more artistic or
useful. His wife runs the Sub Base Players, a theater group
composed of active-duty military and wives of active-duty
military. She's directing and starring in *Auntie Mame*.
When we're back in New London he talks to his wife about
me and she agrees to meet with me.

After bracing my confidence with more than a few drinks at
the Acey Deucy Club on base, I stop by the theater during

rehearsals. After introducing myself and asking if I might join the group, I'm told by the Director to leave and not return if I've been drinking. Embarrassed, I listen, return to rehearsals sober, and get a small part in *Auntie Mame*.

I get a larger role in their next production, *Guys & Dolls*. When one of the lead actors becomes sick with the flu, two days before opening night, I tell the director that I know everyone's lines in  the play and can do that part. She is taken aback for a moment and then decides to run the lines with me. I get the part of Benny South Street for the run of the show and am bitten hard by the theater bug. When I'm about to be released from active duty, the Director gives me a glowing letter of recommendation and suggests I pursue an acting career. That letter will eventually change the course of my life.

Second-Class Citizen

 Because of my issues with authority figures, I'm never gonna be a poster-boy sailor but I love submarines and am a damned good Sonarman. I qualify on submarines and advance from Fireman Apprentice to Petty Officer Second Class Sonarman in less than two years, with no Sonar schooling. I was told that during a war games exercise, our XO commented to the Weapons Officer, "If

it's out there, Giambri'll find it." I muster out at the end of my hitch as Second Class.

I only reach Bear, the second level in Cub Scouts, Second Class in Boy Scouts, and now leave active duty as Second Class in the Navy. Seems that I may be destined to remain second-class in this life.

Tryin' to be a Straight Man

I'm out of the Navy at twenty-three, livin' with my parents back in South Philly, and drinkin' at Ed Mack's again. I'm fixed up on a blind date by my friend Ralph's wife, with what may be the only actual, real blonde in South Philadelphia. A beautiful German-American named Carol. She works at Central Penn National Bank.

Carol and I are made for each other: She's a smart, hot, sexy blonde and I'm a cool dude with a sexy T-bird. We're gonna get married, buy a house in the suburbs, and trade that T-bird for a new, red Corvair Monza SS convertible. We exchange rings. It seems inevitable and perfect.

I just started in the Management Training Program at Philadelphia National Bank, and am attending night school for Stock Transfer Procedures and Commercial Law. I'm wearing three-piece suits and tryin' hard to look like a future bank executive.

I have no way of knowing that I'm just a token ethnic along with the nine other ethnic types in the "training program". Every executive at the bank is a WASP and a Mason. Non-Mason ethnic types will not be in management at this bank for many years to come. I'm makin' $85 a week and tell them I need a $5 raise so that I can get married. I'm told no one in Management Training gets more than a $2 raise. I quit.

In high school, I work after school for a photographer in his darkroom. I love photography and work for nothing to learn how to develop film and make photo prints. I talk my way into a new job as a darkroom technician at a company making parts for the new Apollo Missile System.

After working there for a few months, the company is bought out by a larger corporation, a union shop. We're told by our boss that we have to join the International Brotherhood of Electrical Workers. We're happy with our current situation and tell the boss we'd rather not join any union. He tells us that he and others may get hurt if we refuse to join the union. We get the message and sign up.

Most of our company's factory-line employees are Hispanics who previously worked as pickers on blueberry farms in New Jersey. They don't speak or understand English well and, as a result, I find myself elected Chief Shop Steward in the IBEW at our plant.

I mistakenly take the job seriously and fight to get a contract with better wages for the factory workers. Also, better ventilation near the hazardous chemicals that are used for etching metal parts. Following a particularly contentious meeting with management of the new company and returning to the shop in my old boss's, he tells me that the contract is already "a done deal" and I have to keep my mouth shut or bad things may happen to him and me.

He likes me and saves both our sorry asses by promoting me to a non-union position as Night Manager in the plant so I can't cause problems for him anymore. I'm buried on the midnight to eight shift and made invisible. I make $125 a week but know that I've been fucked. Kinda like Catholic School shit again or the Masons with their fake Management Training Program at the bank. I bite my tongue and carry on.

Philadelphia Drama Workshop

That letter from the Director at The Sub Base Players sits atop my dresser, haunting me until I figure I'll take some weekend acting classes at The Philadelphia Academy of Theater & Acting just for fun.

Carol thinks it's cool until I'm offered a half scholarship to The Philadelphia Drama Workshop Studio, a two-year full-time acting school. The government will pay the other half through the GI Bill, in gratitude for my illustrious military service. When Carol realizes I'm getting serious about acting and may not be the guy she was going to marry, she promptly dumps me for her boss at the bank who seems more likely to fulfill her dreams of suburbia.

Broken-hearted, I quit the factory job and go for the scholarship. Needing pocket money, I accept a job as school janitor. I drink my dinner break with the school carpenter who is also on scholarship and getting government help for service rendered. Without much extra cash, we drink mostly in local dive bars. Tom and I hang together as drinking buddies, acting professionals, and roommates at times. We will be good friends for many years, when we both are a bit more sober, married, and trying to act normal.

Mildred is in my acting classes. She's a very attractive blonde English woman in her late thirties married to a

99

gentleman who owns a girdle factory in Liverpool. She seems to be on the prowl and I pick up the scent. I invite her for a drink at Ed Mack's. The night bartender is my buddy, Harry, who is what's called "punch drunk". His nose is flat from too many breaks, his eyebrows are heavily scarred from healed cuts, and his ears are what were called "cauliflowered". His boxing career did not treat his body well. Harry is a sweet humble guy who always calls everyone "kid", and I love him.

Mildred and I enter Ed Mack's on a Friday night and the joint is rockin'. We take a seat at the bar and Harry greets us with, "What'll it be kids?" I look over at Mildred and asked what she'd like. She says, "A gimlet." I look at her, Harry looks at me, Mildred looks at me with consternation. Harry says, "Lady, we got shots and we got beers. What's it gonna be?" She turns to me with arched eyebrow, gives me "that look," and I know Mildred and I are never gonna happen.

Needing more drinking money, I take on an additional job as janitor at Cinderella Career Schools, an affiliated all-girls secretarial/modeling/airline stewardess school around the corner from acting school. My janitor's office is the only area in the school where smoking's allowed (at my insistence). When not cleaning toilets or mopping floors. I type out stories and poems on an antique Underwood typewriter I commandeer from a storage closet. Students who smoke hang out in my office. They seem impressed that I'm writing poetry and it offers opportunities for someone like me with minimal moral standards. Life is starting to look better.

In my last year of drama school, I'm willfully seduced at a party by fellow student Sandra. Her parents bought her a '61 T-bird convertible with a red leather interior when she graduated high school. She lip-syncs Barbara Streisand in Atlantic City nightclubs and has a following of wanna-be "Sugar Daddies." I have a '60 white T-bird hardtop that I bought cash when leaving the Navy. Two years mostly underwater built a good nest egg. Sandra and I both drive too fast, drink too much, and love acting. We become the Liz Taylor and Richard Burton of our school. We're a continuing subject of gossip among students and staff for our frequent, public outbursts, fights, and drunken party craziness, but when we step on stage together, magic happens.

Our Senior graduation presentation is a concert reading of *John Brown's Body*. I'm one of two featured readers and am made aware that a producer of Italian "spaghetti westerns" is in the audience. Following the performance, our Director tells me privately that this producer has selected me for a feature part in his next movie. It's going to be filmed in Spain in July. I will get "Introducing Phillip Giambri" billing in the credits and my character, although a bad guy, will evoke sympathy when he dies at the end... The kind of part that made Charles Bronson a star. That's pretty much how I anticipated my career starting after graduation.

I'm instructed to get a passport, required medical shots, and be ready to leave in early July. I've already been accepted and signed a contract as an Actors Equity Union apprentice at Hampton Playhouse in New Hampshire for the summer and have to report by Memorial Day weekend. What to do?

One of the few times in my life, I pay attention to my father's advice to go to summer stock and leave if/when I have to go to Spain for the film shoot. Wise advice in the end, as the film is never made because the fading star, who has the lead in the movie is dropped from his contract for "personal reasons" (code for he's an alcoholic on another drinking binge). The movie is never made. Thus, ends my short-lived career as a Charles Bronson wannabe. After this first major letdown, I soon accept that an acting career may prove a lot more difficult to enter than I've been thinking.

Following graduation, Sandra apprentices in summer stock near Boston, and I'm off to Hampton Playhouse to apprentice. Things aren't quite the same between us after that summer. She passes on an STD that she acquired from an affair with an older actor. She is reluctant to admit responsibility for the STD until she too tests positive. I am very slow to forgive. We both move to New York, live separately but continue in a tumultuous, roller-coaster relationship, full of drama, heartache, and "fuck buddy" sex. After seven years, we part as friends when I fall in love and move in with my future wife. Sandra eventually leaves New York. I never see her again.

A Better Man

"Success is going from failure to failure without losing your enthusiasm."

-Winston Churchill.

Hampton Playhouse, 1967

As a twenty-seven-year-old apprentice, I get the opportunity to audition for several small speaking parts and I get to play Scar
Edwards, a Capone-type character in one of the first shows of the season.

I also get to understudy the lead in *The Odd Couple* and perform the role of Oscar on a full house Saturday night. Blythe Danner is the season ingenue. Chevy Chase is an unknown drummer at the time and is dating Blythe. He comes up on weekends to visit occasionally. Sylvia Miles has just finished shooting *Midnight Cowboy* and comes up for several plays. She boasts about actually fucking John Voight in their steamy sex scene and flaunts 8 X 10 glossies as proof. Tony LoBianco is the male lead in most shows this season before becoming well-known in films like *The French Connection, The Honeymoon Killers*, and *The Seven-Ups*.

As an apprentice, I learn the secrets of being a good Stage Manager and this will serve me well in the future. The season's Director likes my work and hires me for the following full summer season at Green Hills Theater in

Reading, PA as a union-contracted actor, with no second-year apprenticeship necessary.

Green Hills Theater

May 1968: Martin Luther King is killed in April, and in a few weeks, Bobby Kennedy is shot. I'm off to a season of summer stock in Reading, PA., where I meet Morrison and Claudia.

Morrison's the lead actor in our theatre company, I'm the season's supporting actor, and Claudia's the foxy-blonde ingénue. Other actors come and go for specific parts, and leave after two weeks. Morrison and I spend off-hours drinking beer, shelling nuts at The Peanut Bar, and swapping life stories. By summer's end, we're "best buds." He's tall, lean, intensely honest, a romantic, and has a brooding, James Taylor kinda' quality that women find irresistible.

Mary is a college student on summer break when she shows up with her sister, who is hired as Prop Mistress and Costumer. Mary tags along as an unpaid assistant on a summer adventure. She's beautiful, blonde, shy, hardworking, humble, and a talented classical pianist. It isn't long before everyone falls in love with her; even those smooth-talkin', successful, New York City, middle-aged actors can't resist her innocence and beauty.

Most of our company live in cheap monastic, cell-like rooms in a downtown hotel while Mary and her sister rent an apartment in an old Victorian house: A perfect spot for after-show parties and gatherings. Mary is serenaded, wooed, gifted, showered with flowers, and invited on dates that she graciously refuses. Her not-so-pretty-older-sister remains in everyone's "friend zone."

Sometime late in the summer, the local newspaper lists me in a review as "Best Supporting Actor" of the season. Easy win for me. I'm the only supporting actor there this season. Mary approaches me at a party, congratulates me, and asks why I never talk to her or bother with her. I'm having an affair with a local lady who owns an antique store but Mary is really who I want to be with all summer. Never for a moment do I think I have a chance with such intense competition from better-looking and more successful cast members. I tell her that and she confesses that she's flattered, but embarrassed by all the attention and has been hoping I'd ask her out. "Rim shot, please!"

The first time we're alone at her place we're makin' out on the living room couch and we're getting very passionate and heated. She says she'd like to make love but she's on her period. Do I mind? Not missing a beat, "I love Bloody Marys." She seems momentarily confused but breaks out in a laugh when she gets it.

I have acting parts in every show except the season's finale, *Who's Afraid of Virginia Wolf*. The company's Stage Manager has to leave before rehearsals for a prior commitment. I volunteer to remain as Stage Manager to close out the season and spend more time with Mary.

On Becoming a New Yorker: 1968-1974

The antique-store lady gifts me an oak church pew and an antique horn speaker. Summer ends and it's back to a new reality in New York City. I'm squatting in a rent-controlled sublet in Spanish Harlem with two Drama Workshop school buddies. We split the $89 a month rent three ways and dine on $.99 six-packs of Rupert beer from the brewery around the corner.

Mary follows shortly but our affair is destined for failure. Her high school sweetheart is serving in Viet Nam and she grows increasingly guilty about our relationship. She cries after lovemaking, finally leaves in tears, and goes back home out West. I never see or hear from her again.

The Fortune Theater and Channel One

Just a bit down from Café La Mama on East 4th Street is the Fortune Theater where a new play is in rehearsals. The first job I get when I arrive in NYC in 1968 is Assistant Stage Manager for this show. I'm recommended by the Green Hills Theater Stage Manager. Below our theater is

107

CHANNEL ONE
UNDERGROUND TELEVISION
OPEN MONDAY, JULY 10th 9 PM

Channel One Underground TV, produced by then-unknown Chevy Chase, who I met at Hampton Playhouse last year when he was Blythe Danner's boyfriend. He had visited regularly but now doesn't remember ever meeting me.

The Channel One show consists of a very long video of a fly walking over a nude woman's body. You have to be really stoned to last through the entire video. The attractive female ushers regularly join us on the fire escape to smoke weed and talk about the catatonic state of the audience.

My primary job in our play "City Scenes" is to operate the sound equipment. It requires accurate queuing of complicated original sound cues and effects. At some point in rehearsals, I'm told that I will also be the off-stage voice of a neighbor in the next apartment and will understudy Michael Douglas and Raul Julia as well. Script lines to be learned for this virtual one-man band! It's an Equity Off-Broadway show and everyone has a union contract except me. When I question the Stage Manager, he assures me I will get one as I'm a member of the Actors Equity Union. Two days before opening, I inform the Director that I won't be attending the opening night without a union contract. It's a very tense and heated few hours before I'm grudgingly given a contract to sign.

A side result of the sound operator part of my job is that the guy who provides the sound equipment for the show works as an IATSE Local 8 Union Sound Man for TV and is a former Shop Steward in Local 8. He likes the way I work the show and is impressed that I did sound work in the military. He takes me on a tour of his union shop and offers me an apprenticeship in the union. Unions are tight and no one gets in without having a family member in the union. His offer is a "chance of a lifetime". Being certain that my acting career will be taking off at any moment, I respectfully decline, "If I take this job and get comfortable as a "techie", then I'll probably pay less attention to my acting career and that's my real goal in life." He laughs loudly and tells me I'm makin' a big mistake. Several years later, I will deeply regret my decision.

Our show opens to bad reviews and closes after sixteen performances but I actually get mentioned for my ten lines in a newspaper review, "Archly narrated by Phillip Giambri".

Michael Douglas is a gracious and patient actor during the rehearsal process for his very first theater appearance. In closing, he gives me his aviator sunglasses from the show and his wardrobe suit. It's a sharp forest green double-breasted suit. We're the same size. I wear that suit to auditions for several years, always feeling that I'll soon be the next Michael Douglas.

La Mama and Me

The summer stock director I worked with for two seasons is directing the first show opening of the newly-renovated Café La Mama, Ross Alexander's "Body of An American."

It's an anti-war play set in a circus theme and stars my buddy, Morrison. I'm wearing a leotard, sporting an afro, and a face made up to  look like a Picasso painting and IT'S LA MAMA!

Morrison runs into Claudia at an open call. There's some electricity and they eventually move in together on the Upper West Side. We're all poor but happy actors. Our world is about to turn upside down and inside out.

The Summer of Love

Rollin' into 1969, we dive headfirst into the counter-culture. Morrison, Claudia, and I hang out a lot listening to Moody Blues, Vanilla Fudge, and The Who's "Tommy." We're smokin' pure Moroccan hash, tripping on mescaline, and rollin' lots of Maui Wowie. Livin' the high life!

I meet a dancer on a commercial shoot and she and I run off to Cape May, NJ, for the summer: Free spirits, teachin' and trippin' in an art commune at the Emlen Physick Estate. We're fighting attempts to  knock it down and build a motel. Just a bunch of mostly-white kids tryin' to save a small piece of the world. Eventually, it will be fully restored and become a Victorian museum. We also help save Lucy the Elephant landmark in Ventnor, NJ. that summer when they try to tear it down. Sometimes the good guys win. Summer ends and it's back to the city.

We're living in her small studio on Washington Place. With no blinds or window shades, we love knowing our neighbor often watches us having sex from his kitchen window. This is my first realization that I may be an exhibitionist. It adds more excitement knowing his wife is having an affair with her tapestry teacher and eagerly shares with us the details of her sexual adventures with him.

I start film school at School of Visual Arts, where most of my time is spent making anti-war signs: "Hell no. We won't go!," "Give peace a chance," "Make love not war'" We're organizing and marching in protests, and getting high on higher education.

The relationship with "Dancer" eventually crashes and burns. She says, "We're done. Ya' gotta' split, man." I'm gone.

Morrison to the Rescue

After a month of couch bouncing and apartment sitting for friends, I give Morrison a buzz. He tells me that he and Claudia were married last summer, exchanged vows in a hippie, tie-dye, and bandana wedding by a lake in New Hampshire. They gave up their place on the Upper West Side for a cheaper one in the East Village. I explain my lack of livin' space, and he says I can crash with him and Claudia at their pad.

I'm sleeping on a homemade platform couch in their cramped living room. Across from me, on a similar platform, sleeps Mellie. She's a friend of Claudia, who just left her husband, an editor for the East Village Other. Morrison and Claudia sleep in a tight loft space he built above the tiny kitchen. It's very claustrophobic and adjustments have to be made by everyone to exist in this confined space.

Morrison works at New Vision building stage sets, and Claudia works as a bored beautician cutting Jane Fonda-style shags all day. Mellie, a dental assistant, is taking an "emotional time out." I'm out of work and sporadically takin' classes at film school. We're both heartbroken and really bummed out.

At night, we all listen to John Lennon records and smoke lots of grass. We endlessly discuss the meaning of Carlos Castaneda's books, whether they're real or fiction, and the social impact of *Easy Rider*.

Morrison and Claudia embrace "Primal Scream Therapy," the "craze" of the moment because John and Yoko are doing it. Mellie and I mostly stay stoned and feel awkward during the loud and angry Scream Therapy sessions. Too freakin' much, man!

Claudia appeals to her building Super for help with our increasingly desperate living situation. They eventually find me a cheap phone-booth-size-studio on St. Marks Place between 2nd and 3rd Avenues. Everybody's cool with that.

Mellie divorces her husband and shacks up with her dentist boss. Morrison and Claudia eventually split up. She moves to Hollywood to pursue her acting career. Last I hear from her, she's livin' with the drummer from Blue Cheer, and working as an assistant to Saul Bellow. She works poolside in a bikini at his luxurious home, bangin' down umbrella drinks, while proofin' his books.

Morrison's still coopin' at the pad on East 9th Street, workin' as a carpenter, dealin' nickel bags on the side. It's there, after a hit of STP, that he experiences an intense religious conversion and becomes "born-again." He joins Hare Krishna and they send him to Florida. I hear from a mutual friend that he's detoxed, shaved his head, and taken a vow of celibacy. "Far fuckin' out, man!", as he always said when he was stoned.

Theater but Not Acting

I work off-Broadway as a techie doing sound, lighting, and stage managing while waiting for my big break. I'm offered a full-time job working in a recording studio owned by a man who rents sound equipment to theater and dance shows I've worked on. He likes my work, hires me, and soon I'm editing sound tapes, recording performers in the studio, and helping with his accounting. His bookkeeping is a mess and he's hemorrhaging money. I tell him I can fix that and now I'm the new Business Manager of G & T

Harris, Inc. We're providing services to Broadway shows, Off-Broadway shows, and all the major NYC dance companies. We franchise an innovative slide-show sync that allows us to automate slide shows with up to three projectors; an innovative piece of equipment for the times. We also record the very popular "Dial-a-Joke" for AT&T and get to work with the country's top comedians. My boss is happy, we're out of the red, and we're making money.

A Poor Player Strutting and Fretting

From the moment I accept the scholarship to acting school, I become totally committed to becoming a working actor. I never expect to be "a star" but do want to build a reputation as a good working actor in theater and film.

Once in New York, I do everything an aspiring actor is expected to do: I get an answering service, headshot, resume, trade papers, and religiously "make the rounds" of agent's offices and "call for actors" in the trade papers. Despite becoming friends with workers in producers' and agent's offices, I very seldom get past leaving a pic and resume and a brief chat.

My acting school buddy is now my roommate and he's investing very little time and effort into getting work but continues to be called to audition for commercials and theater parts. I have to concede that as a six-foot-four good-looking Irish-American, he's a lot more in demand than a five-foot-eight "swarthy" Italian-American. He's admittedly not a very good actor, chokes at auditions, and doesn't really get any work.

I begin auditioning for union-approved "Showcases" where Equity actors can display their talent to potential agents and producers. Over several years, I gain a reputation as a good actor who works for free. I look at it as a learning opportunity and a chance to meet other professional actors. It becomes more difficult to attend daytime rehearsals and evening showcases while earning $3.50 an hour working nights. I'm putting in and taking out Off-Broadway shows opening and closing. I also become adept at running lights for Off-Broadway shows and have more offers than time.

In 1969, Broadway is not doing well. Off-Broadway and Off-Off-Broadway are taking off like fireworks downtown. The Local 8 Stagehands Union decides they're out of work members can get jobs by Unionizing Off-Broadway into Local 8. This does not sit well with those of us eking out a living working staff and tech Off-Broadway. We arrange a meeting of Off-Broadway workers and decide the only option we have is to start our own union. A framework for The League of Off-Broadway Theatrical Employees and Technicians is drawn up and we begin handing out flyers at every Off-Broadway theater. Local 8 soon becomes aware of our plan and decides to offer Local 8 union cards to those of us who are leading the formation of LOBTET, our own union. Not being stupid, we know that accepting Local 8 cards will kill our attempts at unionizing and that we'll never be offered real jobs on Broadway. As a group, we tell them to "fuck off!" We continue with our plans to unionize while several new musicals are opening on Broadway to rave reviews. With the seeming revival of Broadway jobs, Local 8 loses interest in working downtown with hippies. We dissolve our non-union and continue working at slave wages but we're proud of our success in organizing.

Broadway Bound

The Director who gave me my union card in summer stock and my first acting job in New York City at La Mama Café is now about to direct a Broadway show. He calls and tells me he has a great character part for me and I'll be onstage the entire show. He promises I will be noticed.

I show up for the audition and to my surprise, in addition to my Director-friend, is the show's Producer, who I know well and do business with at G & T Harris. He looks at me in disbelief, shakes my hand, and says, "Phil, really? Seriously?"

I do a good and credible audition and leave thanking everyone. The Director calls the next day to tell me that my Producer-friend liked my audition but is not willing to go with a lead character who's never done a Broadway show before. The Director insists he wants me for the part and calls me in for a second audition in front of the Producer, which I nail.

Long story short, after a third audition at the Director's request, the Producer is still unwilling to hire his "techie" buddy for a lead Broadway part. The show opens to mixed reviews and closes after two weeks. I swear I never put a curse on that show, but am not at all unhappy when it closes.

I manage to get day work in movies as an extra, get a few jobs a bit higher up with screen time, and get to work with a few famous actors who don't notice me.

An agent's office manager, who I've become friendly with over several years, offers this advice: "You're a good actor but you don't have "the look" that's in now. You're not a Robert Redford type and you won't get calls for commercials or most film parts. You're gonna be a good character actor and will get a lot of work if you can hang in for ten or fifteen years until you're the right age for that kinda' work." WOW! I respond, "What the fuck am I supposed to do until then? Work for $3.50 an hour?" He suggested I try to find a "real" job.

I'm disillusioned and depressed but also realize that he's telling me the truth as he sees it. I continue making the rounds and doing auditions but my heart just isn't in it anymore. Through a friend in an advertising agency, I get a job reviewing resumes and interviewing actors for TV commercials. It's not long before I realize that the agency has a list of actors that they regularly use and who their sponsors like. The interviews I'm doing are merely to give the appearance of fair play and compliance with the law. Disgusted, I quit and return to theater tech work where at least people are more honest.

Soho Rent Parties

In the early '70s, there's lots of empty commercial space between Houston and Canal Streets along Lafayette and Broadway. Artists begin taking over these large empty floors for studios and living spaces. It is not uncommon to see flyers in bookstores and on street poles advertising a "Rent Party" at a loft downtown. Sometimes we just hear about a party from people on the street. I only go to two but they're memorable.

My first Rent Party is at a loft on Lafayette Street. I take a freight elevator to the third floor along with about a dozen others. The elevator opens to an immense space that runs an entire block on Lafayette Street and is about fifty feet wide. There's a pretty lady by the elevator collecting two bucks from each person to cover the rent.

One wall is lined with Altec Voice of the Theatre speakers, normally used at outdoor rock concerts. They're spaced along the wall about every ten feet. Jumpin' Jack Flash is playing and there is a wall of sound coming from the speakers that vibrate the walls, the floors, and everyone there. I can feel the cells in my body vibrating. One hundred or more people are moving and vibrating to music so loud, you feel it as much as hear it. I have to dance. I dance and keep on dancing for hours. There's no visible alcohol here but a thick fog of pot smoke permeates the space. It feels like this is what you'd want heaven to be.

About a month later, I see a flyer on the bulletin board at the East Side Book Store for another Rent Party. My buddy Helmut and I have been doin' a heavy, happy hour at Holiday Cocktail Lounge and are pretty buzzed. We decide to skip dinner, pick up a slice on the way, and head downtown to the address on the flyer. There's a freight elevator full of people and we get off as the doors open to an extremely large square space seemingly filled to capacity. We're charged a very small admission fee and directed to the coatroom. It's twice the size of my apartment, but with no coatracks or hangers. The coats are all stacked in a gigantic pile almost filling the room. We chuck our coats in the pile and head over to the main room.

Everyone's dancing to very loud rock music and Helmut and I are scouting the room for attractive girls who can dance and seem unattached. We spot two young ladies who are dancing together. One is short, very pretty, and dressed mostly in black leather everything. Her friend is a Cher-look-alike dressed in flowing hippie tie-dye and she's barefoot. Helmut is a much smoother talker than me, even with his German accent. We walk over to the ladies and he opens the conversation. The "leather lady" is a well-known, downtown, pre-Punk songwriter, bodybuilder, artist, and local cool chick. Her friend is a graphic designer living and working in the West Village. We manage to pass ourselves off as a bit hipper than we actually are and spend a few hours doing some hard dancing until we're all exhausted and sweaty. We retreat to the coatroom, dive into a pile of coats and both couples begin heavy makin' out for what seems like hours. We all leave together, with each couple headed to the lady's apartment, to top off another great downtown adventure. Helmut and I meet for lunch the next day. All we have to say is, "Fuck, YEAH!" and laugh long and loud.

I'm soon in a living situation with two sisters, out of work, broke, and settling for whatever entertainment we can muster up in my apartment. No more loft parties for this boy.

Bunny of the Year

I end my career at G & T Harris, Inc. as the Technical Coordinator for the 1972 Playboy Bunny of the Year contest in Vernon Valley Great Gorge, NJ. It's a cluster-fuck! Most of the Playboy production staff are blitzed on amphetamines the whole time and my drug-free crew and I are criticized for not working fast enough or hard enough.

We work tirelessly and the show gets on, but that too is problematic. Dick Shawn, the show host, is stuck in NYC and I have to drive in to pick him up. Then, Heff's plane is delayed and Dick has to ad-lib for two hours until Heff finally arrives. The lady who wins is disliked by all the other contestants and, by our crew, during rehearsals and interview events.

What should have been a hard-working fun week turns out to be exhausting and disappointing. Not a career-maker for sure; however, I leave with a suitcase full of Playboy merch. It's all eventually stolen by invited friends of my girlfriend, Selena, at a party she has in my apartment when I'm on tour with a show.

Selena & Sista

I hook up with Selena in an acting class. We're soon living together in my tiny apartment across from the Electric Circus. We take in her sister who was evicted from her apartment and homeless. We sleep packed tightly on the floor, on cushions from a rocking chair I rescued from the trash. Sister Lisa gets a job at Baskin Robbins on 8th street, decorating ice cream cakes. She always makes one with disgusting color combinations, so it won't sell and brings it home for us to eat. We have very little money and that's our dinner most nights.

Selena is beautiful. Her pussy tastes briny, sweet, and as delicious as a West Coast Oyster. Our sex is good and I soon find myself falling in love with her. She, on the other hand, is a free spirit only interested in friendship, casual sex, and a place to hang out for a while. After several months living at my place, she tells me she's slept with my friend David Wilke, who will soon become East Village legend, Adam Purple. I'm hurt but silent. Selena never notices but her sister does and offers consolation. Selena eventually takes off for Canada to live in a tent with some blonde hippie guy she meets at a concert in Central Park.

Soon after Selena leaves, Lisa gets raped in Tompkins Square Park one late night, hangs around for several months to heal emotionally, then joins the Army. I learn from her letters that she works in Army Intelligence and marries a fellow serviceman, who becomes a professional wrestler and physically abuses her. She leaves him and returns to live with her mother in Philadelphia. She tells me Selena joined The Inner Peace Movement and is running a boarding house for their members in the mid-West somewhere.

I Am Woman

Paul, who runs the acting class where I met Selena, knows of my reputation as a good theater soundman. He's directing a new one-woman show starring theater and film actress, Viveca Lindfors. On the very sunrise of the women's liberation movement, *I Am Woman* is the right show for this moment: It's comprised of women's monologues from a large selection of famous plays and will have a complicated soundtrack on tape. The show is going on tour; changes in the order of monologues are occurring after every rehearsal, and are expected to continue. He asks me to handle the complicated daily sound editing and operate the sound equipment during performances on tour.

I'm presently out of work and decide to take the job 'cause the money's good, I like Director Paul, and the tour sounds like fun. I do and it is: The show rides the crest of the wave of the woman's liberation movement!

I spend countless hours on the road with Viveca, as chauffer, gofer, dinner companion, escort, sounding board, and shoulder to lean on, as well as Sound Man and occasionally Stage Manager. She lives in a brownstone not far from me with her son, Kristopher, also an actor. I run into her near the subway station about a year after we finish touring. She acts like she doesn't know me and ignores my hello. That's "Show Biz." I guess.

Frau Regina

It's New Year's Eve and my Algerian friend, Brahim, invites me to join him at an uptown, international nightclub populated mostly by Euro Trash with money. I tag along without any expectations and ring in the New Year, kissing a cute blonde German girl, who tells me she's always mistaken for Elke Somer. I don't' see that at all, but long story short, she moves in with me, cooks seven-course meals every night, and we polish off two six-packs of Lowenbrau Octoberfest every day.

She insists I read Der Spiegel aloud so that I can learn German. She often comments that my German sounds more Swiss and I sound too delicate and gay. Her dedication is not completely in vain. I learn and remember one significant and useless sentence in German that was never in Der Spiegel: "Du hast einen knutschfleck am hals!" which means, "You have a hickey on your neck."

Regina and I never really click emotionally or physically and love never comes up. She takes up with my German bar buddy, Helmut, by mutual agreement of all. They live together for several years before she runs off with an elevator repairman at Bonwit Teller, where she works. Wonder if he had a hickey on his neck.

The Naked Airline Stewardess

She lives on the top floor of my building across from my friends, Marie and Jerry. She's a Senior Stewardess for American Airlines and flies back and forth to Mexico City several times a week. When home, she's always naked and her apartment door is always open. Flaming red hair both above and below.

Following a brief fling with my friend, Arthur, she decides to give me a try. Seems she has "daddy issues" though. We have to make love on daddy's bed. It's the one he was born on and she talks excessively about her daddy, a congressman, before and after sex. She also reveals she's never had an orgasm.

After a month or two of Herculean effort, I have to concede that I will not be the guy who brings her to ecstasy, as long as she insists on directing and dominating every move during our lovemaking. It's no wonder she can't climax; she's too busy directing! When I point this out on several occasions, she determines that, despite my intense efforts, I may not be the guy who can make her climax for Daddy on his bed.

We remain friends until she's fired from her job for being marginally overweight. She insists that men her height are permitted heavier weight and that it's unfair. She loses her case in court and moves to San Francisco, never to be heard from again. Is she searching for that ever-elusive Daddy-Climax on the West Coast now? I hope she finds it there. She was sweet and a lot of fun.

Days of Wine and Roses

I'm out of work for the summer, collecting "a government subsidy to the arts" or NYS Unemployment, as it's officially known. I spend a lot of time hangin' out in front  of my building at 26 St. Marks Place, across from the Electric Circus. With me regularly is my neighbor, Marie, who is also out of work. We smoke a lot of weed, drink cheap Spanish wine, and watch the freak parade go by all day.

I'm also hangin' nights at Grassroots Tavern, just a few doors from my place. I seem to be havin' a hard time hookin' up with ladies who don't give me STDs. Marie laughs every time I tell her my latest misadventures with the Grassroots gals. She says she and her husband have a friend from college coming to town while waiting on her divorce to be finalized. Says her name is Loislee but everybody calls her Curly. I ask what she looks like and

Marie says, "Just your type: Blonde hair and big tits!" "Hey, I'm in!"

On our first date, I take her to the midnight show of *Reefer Madness* at the St. Marks Theater on 2nd Avenue. We eat popcorn and smoke a few doobies while deciding whether or not we're likin' each other. It takes only two more dates before we know we're in love and soon become inseparable.

We decide to live together and find a larger apartment on St. Marks Place between 1st and 2nd Avenues. We have forty-two wonderful years together on St. Marks Place.

Truckin' on Saint Marks Place

I had no way of knowing at the time, but that first *Summer of Love* in '69 marked the beginning of my incredible fifty-two-year *Magical Mystery Tour* on St. Marks Place! I'm still here, it's still magical, and I just keep on truckin'!

125

The Cowboy Code

Live each day with courage.

Take pride in your work.

Always finish what you start.

Do what has to be done.

Be tough, but be fair.

When you must make a promise, keep it.

Ride for the brand.

Talk less, say more.

Remember that some things aren't for sale.

Know where to draw the line.

One of my favorite speeches comes from Robert Duvall in "Second Hand Lions":

"Sometimes the things that may or may not be true are the things that a man needs to believe in the most. That people are basically good. That honor, courage and virtues mean everything. That power and money, money and power mean nothing; that Good always triumphs over Evil; and I want you to remember this: That Love, true Love never dies. Doesn't matter if any of this is true or not. You see a man should believe in these things because these are the things worth believing in."

About the Author

Phillip Giambri aka **"The Ancient Mariner"** left home at eighteen and never looked back. He's seen and done what others dream of or fear. That's how he lives and that's what he writes.

His 2020 novelette *The Amorous Adventures of Blondie and Boho* is a story of love, survival, and gentrification in NYC's East Village. The chapbook *Poems from an Unending Pandemic* offers his perspective on NYC life during the COVID-19 pandemic. His 2017 chapbook *Love Borne in Retrograde* is a collection of love poems and erotica and the 2016 novelette *Confessions of a Repeat*

Offender is a compilation of his performance stories and poems.

Phillip is a 2020 Acker Award recipient for Storytelling and Community Service. His work has appeared in *From Somewhere to Nowhere: The End of the American Dream* (Unbearables Anthology 2017), *Eternal Snow: A Worldwide Anthology of 100 Poets* with Yuyutsu Sharma, *Home Planet News* (Issues #2,#5 and #8), *Sensitive Skin Magazine, Artists in the Kitchen, "Walt's Corner"* (The Long Islander), *Silver Birch Press, NewYorkCityTalking.com* and the prestigious *Revista de traduceri literare (Review of Literary Translations) #5 and #56* (Bucharest, Romania).

He has been featured in a 2016 *New York Times* story, *The Villager, Chelsea New*s, and in 2017 on WBAI FM Radio - *"Talk Back"* with Corey Kilgannon. He was also a featured poet at the historic Club A in Bucharest, Romania.

Phillip produced and curated a popular, monthly spoken word/poetry series, *Rimes of The Ancient Mariner,* for five years, was Associate Producer in the Off-Broadway production of *"Intrusion"* (written and performed by Qurrat Ann Kadwani), as well as special collaborative events with other artist/performers: *Barflies & Broken Angels, What the Hell Is Love?, The Losers Club, Are You Dangerous, What Were the '60s Really like?, New York Story Exchange,* and *10 Penny Comedy Show.*
https://www.amazon.com/Phillip-Giambri/e/B01ACGQ7HQ?ref_=dbs_p_pbk_r00_abau_00 0000

Made in the USA
Middletown, DE
28 September 2022

11420980R00076